SELECTED ESSAYS

THE
SEAGULL
LIBRARY OF
GERMAN
LITERATURE

SELECTED ESSAYS

Friedrich Dürrenmatt

TRANSLATED BY

ISABEL FARGO COLE

LONDON   NEW YORK   CALCUTTA

This publication was supported by a grant
from the Goethe-Institut India

Seagull Books, 2019

The original German-language essays appeared in the volumes
Literatur und Kunst; *Theater*; *Politik*; *Philosophie und Naturwissenschaft*;
and *Verusche / Kants Hoffnung, Der Sturz / Abu Chanifa und Anan ben
David / Smithy / Das Sterben der Pythia* by Friedrich Dürrenmatt

© Diogenes Verlag AG, Zurich, Switzerland, 1998

First published in English translation by Seagull Books, 2013

ISBN 978 0 85742 711 3

British Library Cataloguing-in-Publication Data
A catalogue record for this book is available from the British Library.

Typeset by Seagull Books, Calcutta, India
Printed and bound by WordsWorth India, New Delhi, India

CONTENTS

FROM THE BEGINNING

1957

I was born on 5 January 1921 in Konolfingen (Canton of Bern). My father was a pastor, my paternal grandfather a politician and poet in the town of Herzogenbuchsee. He composed a title poem for each issue of his newspaper. For one such poem he spent ten days in prison. 'Ten days for ten stanzas, and I bless every day,' he later wrote. So far I haven't had that honour. Perhaps it's me or perhaps our age has gone to the dogs and doesn't even feel offended when railed against. My mother (whom I resemble) comes from a pretty village near the mountains. Her father was mayor and patriarch. The town where I was born and grew up isn't pretty, a conglomeration of urban and rural buildings, but the surrounding villages, which belonged to my father's parish, were (and are to this day) genuine Emmental, like something from Jeremias Gotthelf.[1] It's a land in which milk plays the main role. The farmers take it in big vats to Stalden AG, the milk-pasteurization plant at the centre of town. My first encounter with art was in Konolfingen. My sister and I sat for the town painter. From then on I spent hours painting and drawing in the master's studio. My motifs—floods and Swiss battles. I was a warlike child. As a six-year-old I often ran about the garden armed with a long beanpole and a pot

[1] Jeremias Gotthelf (1797–1854): Classic Swiss writer best known for his novella *The Black Spider* (1842).

lid as a shield, reporting to my mother at last in exhaustion that the Austrians had been expelled from the garden. When my warlike deeds took to paper, covering the patient surface with ever-bloodier battles, my mother turned in alarm to the painter Cuno Amiet, who studied the gory sheets in silence before pronouncing curtly, 'One day he'll be a colonel.' Here the master was mistaken—in the Swiss army I ranked only as an auxiliary, in life I rank only as a writer. I won't describe here the further tracks, right and wrong, that brought me here. But in my present occupation I have salvaged important things from the world of my childhood—not only my first impressions, not only the model for my present world, but also the 'method' of my art itself. In the local artist's studio painting appeared to me as a craft, a plying of brush, charcoal, pen, etc. Likewise, writing for me today is an engagement and experiment with different materials. I grapple with theatre, radio, novels and television, and from my grandfather I know that writing can be a form of fight.

The story of my writing is the story of my materials. Materials, however, are impressions transformed. You write as a whole man, not as a man of letters, much less as a grammarian; everything is connected because everything is brought into relation, everything can turn out to be so important, decisive, usually in retrospect, unsuspected. Stars are concentrations of interstellar matter, writing is the concentration of impressions. No evasion is possible. As you are the result of your environment, you must own up to it, but the crucial impressions are made in your youth, the lingering horror that seized me when the greengrocer in his little shop beneath the theatre hall parted the leaves of a lettuce with his handless arm. We are formed by such impressions; what comes later joins preformed things, is processed according to a predetermined pattern, assimilated to the pre-existing, and the stories we heard as children are more crucial than literature's influences. This grows clear to us when we look back. I am not a village writer, but the village brought me forth, and so I am still a slow-talking villager, not a city person, a big-city person least of all, even if I couldn't live in a village any more.

The village itself formed at the intersection of the roads from Bern to Lucerne and Burgdorf to Thun, on a high plain, at the foot of a big hill, not far from the gallows mound where it's said the officers of the local court once carted the murderers and rabble-rousers. A stream flows across the plain, and the little farming villages and hamlets upon it needed a focal point. The aristocrats in the vicinity had fallen on hard times, their residences converted into old-age or rest homes. First, it seems, there was just a pub at the intersection. Then, diagonally opposite, came the smithy, and later the two other quadrants of this coordinate plane were occupied by the cooperative store and the theatre hall, which was not insignificant, as the village boasted a prominent dramatist, the teacher Gribi, whose plays were performed by dramatic societies throughout Emmental, and even a Yodel King by the name of Schmalz. Along the road to Thun the printer, the cloth dealer, the butcher, the baker and the school set up shop, the last almost at the edge of the next farming village, whose boys roughed me up on the way to school and whose dogs we feared, while the parsonage, the church, the cemetery and the savings bank ended up on a slight rise between the road to Thun and the road to Bern. But it was the large milk pasteurization plant, Stalden AG, built on the steep climbing road to Burgdorf, which first made the village into a rural centre; all the area's milk was hauled in, on heavy trucks which we waited for in groups, later, when we had to go to secondary school in Grosshöchstetten, hanging on to them and letting them tow us up the road to Burgdorf on our bikes, scared to death, not of the police—we all felt capable of coping with the fat village policeman—but of the French and writing teacher we called Baggel, whose lessons we dreaded, malicious beater, pincher and hair-puller that he was, even forcing us to shake each other's hands, the *Grüss Gott* of educated Europeans, and clinging to one another behind the clattering truck with the dancing, morning-empty milk cans, we pictured the teacher as a huge mountain we had to scale, with grotesque toponyms and accordingly difficult climbs. But that was already shortly before I moved to the city; in my recollection the train station is more important than the milk pasteurization plant with its smokestack, which more than the church steeple served as the village landmark. It had the right to call itself a train station because it was a railway junction, and we villagers were proud of it—only a few trains were bold enough not to stop, roaring past towards distant Lucerne, towards closer-by Bern; sitting on a bench outside the station building, I often awaited them with a mixture of longing and loathing before they steamed past and away. But memory slips back still further into the underpass where the train tracks crossed the road to Burgdorf, from which stairs led straight to the train station. It appears to me as a dark cave into which I strayed as a three-year-old, in the middle of the road, having absconded from home to the village; at the end of the cave was sunlight out of which the dark shadows of the cars and wagons loomed but it is no longer clear where in fact I was heading, as the underpass led not only to the milk pasteurization plant and the train station, the slope of the Ballenbühl was also home to the higher-class people such as my godmother, the wife of the village doctor, to whom I later had to bring my never-satisfactory school reports for perusal, the parish president, the dentist and the dental technician. The two of them ran the Dental Institute, which maltreats broad swathes of the region to this day and makes the village famous. They owned cars, which itself was enough to make them privileged, and in the evening they piled together the money earned by filling teeth, pulling teeth and manufacturing dentures and divided it by hand without counting it. The dental technician was short and fat; occupied with issues of public health, he had a health bread made that curdled the blood. But the dentist was an imposing man and a French speaker, probably from Neuchâtel. He was thought to be the richest man in the entire district; later this belief was revealed to be a tragic misapprehension. But he was certainly the most pious, member of an extreme sect who talked about Christ as he drilled, his religious zeal matched only by a gaunt woman who always wore black, visited, as she claimed, by the angels, who read the Bible even while milking and to whom I had to bring the peddlers and vagrants across the plain from the parsonage to be put up at night, for my parents ran a hospitable parsonage and turned no one away and shared our meals with whomever wished, such as the children of a circus that visited the village once a year. And once a Negro turned up. Jet black, he sat at the family table to my father's left and ate rice with tomato sauce. He was converted, but I was afraid anyway. All in all much conversion went on in the village. Revival meetings were held in tents, the Salvation Army marched in, sects formed, evangelists preached, but the village's greatest claim to fame in this regard was the Muslim mission which had its headquarters in a palatial chalet high above the village, for it published a map of the world on which only one place in Europe was named, this village, a piece of missionary pomposity that induced the momentary delusion of living at the centre of the universe and not in a dump in Emmental. That is not too strong a word. The village itself was homely, a cluster of buildings in lower-middle-class style such as one finds throughout the Central Plateau, but the surrounding farming villages with their big roofs and painstakingly layered manure piles were lovely, the dark fir forests all round were mysterious and the plain was full of adventure, with the sorrel in the meadows and the vast grain fields in which we snuck around, building our nests deep within, while the farmers stood at the edges and peered in, cursing. More mysterious still were the dark passageways in the hay which the farmers had stacked on their barn floors, we spent hours crawling round in the warm, dusty darkness and peering down from the openings into the stall where the cows stood in long rows. But for me the spookiest place was the topmost, the windowless attic in my parents' house. It was filled with old newspapers and books that glimmered whitish in the dark. And I had a scare in the washhouse once—a creepy animal lay there, perhaps a salamander—while the cemetery was free of dread. We often played hide-and-seek there, and when a grave had been dug I made myself at home there until the approaching funeral procession, heralded by pealing bells, chased me off. For we were intimate not just with death but with killing. A village has no secrets, and people are predators, with occasional rudiments of humanity that must be dropped at the butcher's. We often watched the journeymen butchers kill, we saw the blood gush from the big animals, we saw them die and be carved up. We children watched, fifteen minutes, half an hour, and then we went back to playing marbles on the sidewalk.

But that is not enough. A village is not the world. Though destinies may unfold there, tragedies and comedies, it is the world that defines the village, leaves it in peace, forgets it or destroys it, and not the other way round. The village is an arbitrary point in the totality of the world, no more than that, significant for nothing, coincidental, interchangeable. The world is larger than the village. Over the woods the stars are suspended. Early on, I made their acquaintance, traced their constellations: the fixed Pole Star; the Little Bear and the Great Bear with the coiled dragon between them; I came to know bright Vega, sparkling Altair, nearby Sirius, distant Deneb, the gigantic sun Aldebaran, the still mightier Betelgeuse and Antares; I knew that the village was a part of the Earth and the Earth a part of the solar system, that the Sun with its planets moved round the centre of the Milky Way towards Hercules, and I learnt that the Andromeda Nebula, barely visible to the naked eye, was a Milky Way like our own. I was never a Ptolemaic. Starting from the village I knew the immediate surroundings, the nearby city, a vacation spa also in the nearby mountains and a few miles of school trips besides, that was all, but up above, in space, a scaffold of vast distances reared up and so it was too with time—the distant was more potent than the immediate. The immediate was perceived only insofar as it entered the tangible realm, as the actual life of the village; even village politics were too abstract, abstracter still were the politics of the country, the social crises, the bank failures which cost my parents their savings, the peace efforts, the Nazis' rise, all too vague, too imageless, but the Flood, that was comprehensible, a vivid event, the wrath of God and the passing of his water, he dumped out the entire ocean over humanity, now go on and swim, and then brave David, boastful Goliath, the adventures of Hercules, the strongest man who ever was, kingly Theseus, the Trojan War, the dark Nibelungs, radiant Dietrich von Bern, the valiant Swiss confederates, thrashing the Austrians and succumbing to vastly superior numbers at St Jakob an der Birs, all held together—the womb of the village and the wild world outside, history and the equally real sagas, but also the immeasurable forms of the universe—by a shadowy Good Lord whom you had to worship, ask forgiveness, but from whom, as from an enigmatic super-uncle behind the clouds, you could also expect kindness, the fulfilment of hopes and wishes. Good and evil were fixed, you found yourself in a perpetual examination, with marks, as it were, for every deed, and that was why school was such a bitter thing—it perpetuated the heavenly system on earth and for the children the adults were demigods. Terrible, beautiful children's land—the world of experience was small, a paltry village, no more; the world of hearsay was huge, floating in an enigmatic cosmos, mingled with a wild fantasy realm of heroic battles, impossible to verify. You had to take this world as it was. You were delivered up to faith, defenceless and naked.

As time progresses, the web in which it snares us grows denser and denser. The very first girl I fell in love with came from Neuchâtel. She was called Claudine, or something else entirely, and she was beautiful. I was just eight, or maybe even seven, and my love was not returned. I resented my age, and so it is really only this resentment I recall, not the object of my love, who was seventeen, eighteen or even twenty, a young woman. She stayed with us on vacation, dressed in white, sitting at a table in our garden and reading. The table stood by a fir I would climb, eager for insights. I first came to Neuchâtel itself in June 1940, as the Germans overran France. I was cycling from Bern and had to get to La Tourne, north of Rochefort, to stay with a pastor and his many children and improve my French—to this day I haven't succeeded. Aside from being broadened, the road from Bern to Neuchâtel has remained essentially unchanged (if you don't take the highway towards Murten), though next to the old wooden bridge in Gümmenen there's a new bridge now, in Gurbrü the curves are gone and on the plain past Kerzers the poplars that lined the road have long been felled. Vanished too is the old road from the Ziehl to St Blaise, which I recall as very narrow, skirting a long wall. Of Neuchâtel itself, as it was back then, I've retained the impression of an endless street that led uphill; it must have been the rue de l'Ecluse, which worms its way up between the castle cliff and the southern foot of the Jura towards Peseux and Corcelles. The midday heat was intense as I pushed my bike up the hill; the last of Corcelles' houses are still standing today. I never guessed that I would return to Neuchâtel twelve years later. My maternal roots might have aroused my suspicions but they were too complicated and I never gave them much thought, learning only recently from my ninety-year-old aunt, my mother's sister, that my grandmother—who had married my grandfather, a widower with children, as a widow with children—came from Neuchâtel, where she and her two sisters had landed, and that a nephew of my grandmother had moved to the Dutch East Indies and become the conductor of a military band, though his artistic career came to an abrupt end; he decided, overcome by homesickness, to return to Neuchâtel but following his farewell concert in Bandung or Surabaya or some other Javanese city, his wife, a native, poisoned him. The grand-nephew was clearly much loved, and by way of my maternal great-grandfather and great-grandmother the genes that had already worked their mischief with him had a hand in me as well, if genes can be said to have hands, and if the conductor had children it's conceivable that still more of these shared genes are knocking about in Java. The saga, like all sagas, is murky, and in the background a family by the name of d. P. crops up as well, possibly de Pury, according to my aunt, who still owns a few heirlooms with these initials. But I'm not the only one who's somehow, somewhere, a Neuenburger. One of the country's sperm banks is located on the road from Neuchâtel to Valangin. Big, clean stables, an administrative building, the waiting room for clients—the human ones—just like at the dentist. Catalogues lie about. Outside farmers are taking a tour. Primordial sounds can be heard through the window—the mighty bulls are trotting round in an oval beneath a roof, about thirty of them, each with a ring in his nostrils connected by a chain to a conveyor beneath the roof. They trot round for an hour like this. Once they are unchained, the bull keepers lead them into the hall. The contraption with the 38°C bag doesn't look like a cow but the bull takes it for one, the bag as warm as a bovine vagina, it takes just seconds, hop to it, the test tube at the end of the bag is replaced and already the next colossus mounts, hop to it, until all the bulls have spent themselves while outside more bulls trot round in an oval beneath the roof, hollowly lowing. After each mount the test tube with the precious liquid is passed through a window into the laboratory. While things in the hall, under the commands of the bull keepers, are rough and rude, almost military, as though in a technological bull brothel, a different atmosphere prevails in the laboratory, the work is not just scientific and clinical but nimble and feminine, the female lab technicians in their white coats impressive as they label the test tubes, enter the numbers into a log, take samples of the stuff of male potency, slide the glass plates with the slick of semen under the microscope—a tail-wagging swarm, the bearers of the genes programmed with the qualities promised by the catalogue. One ejaculation contains 6.8 billion sperm cells; the lab technicians check if it is abundant enough to be used, and if the bull is fit, if the sperm count is good, everything following the sample is fully automated. Twenty-five million sperm are required for artificial insemination (I'm citing this from memory); a bull can produce around two hundred and fifty potential cattle with one thrust into the artificial vagina. The lab technicians and apparatuses are still at work as the bulls, their day's labour done, recline in their vast stalls; one treads softly past these vigorous colossuses, their performance awe-inspiring. For there is something Nordic, Valhalla-like, about the stables, a good place to rest, you'd like to lie down by the heroes.

But somewhat apart from the mighty buildings, as though hidden away, stands a little stall, more a hut, housing one whose semen is harvested only rarely—a brown bearded billy goat of primordial dignity, stinking like hell, both shunned and venerated, a mixture of Pan and the Devil, a sperm producer to whom, in a fit of animal-loving humanity, in appreciation of his solitary singularity, they gave a nanny goat, and truly, the couple reminds me of Philemon and Baucis. Not far from this idyll we have been living for a bit more than a quarter-century now in a little valley up above Neuchâtel, in the Vallon de l'Ermitage, enticed there by a letter offering a house with a 'built-in library' for sale. The joiner was still working in the house when we moved in, there was no electricity yet, and I made soup in the laundry room. The road past our house climbs up Chaumont Mountain along the forest edge and vanishes into the woods. The little valley is closed off by a cliff ridge, the Rocher de l'Ermitage, which gave the valley its name. At its foot are several shallow caves or, rather, broad niches, some facing the valley, where students from the university and commercial college carouse in the summer nights. Then all hell breaks loose. Wild talking, singing, later drunken caterwauling. The girls shriek. The loudest are the German-Swiss. They've come to Neuchâtel to learn French, resulting in the Swiss-German patois known as Français fédéral. Occasionally a religious group also makes its presence felt in the caves—then 'Jésus, sauve-moi!'[1] resounds, followed by long-drawn-out aves, hosannas, amens; the 'Jésus, donne-moi le silence'[2] which I once hollered up there had no effect. In the fifteenth century a Nicolas de Bruges is said to have lived as a hermit in one of these caves, evidently only intermittently

1 'Jesus, save me.'

2 'Jesus, leave me in silence.'

plagued by piety, as he still kept a residence in Neuchâtel and produced gunpowder. Otherwise little historical knowledge about the valley has survived. Around 1692, an Abraham Amiest reported that the Jewish cemetery was situated there but the pious Queen Bertha, who at the end of the ninth century ruled over the kingdom of High Burgundy in Payerne, then called Peterlingen, on the other side of Lake Neuchâtel, banished the Jews from Neuchâtel 'sans jamais leur permettre d'y rentrer'.[3] After the cemetery vanished, the vineyards must have reached up to the cliff, judging by the crumbling terrace walls. Several centuries later, the little valley may have come into the possession of the Merveilleux, whose real name was Wunderlich and whose progenitor Hans Wunderlich was cook to the Count of Neuchâtel around 1430; indeed, overall, the area seems to bring forth culinary proclivities; in prehistoric times, before the Celts came, the first inhabitants of the lakeshore are said to have been cannibals, as doubtless were we all in the dim, dark past. When the counts of Neuchâtel died out, the little land ended up with the house of Orléans-Longueville. When this too went extinct, the 'King in Prussia', Frederick I,[4] inherited the princedom, backed on the one hand by a legal assessment from the philosopher Leibnitz[5] and encouraged on the other by the politics of Neuchâtel's chancellor, Georges de Montmollin, one of whose descendants—he has many—lives at the bottom of the valley at the top of which I live. In 1848 Neuchâtel liberated itself from Prussia and declared itself a republic; whether as an inevitable result of this new order it 'lapsed back into barbarism', as prophesied

---

3 'Without ever allowing them to return.'

4 Frederick I (1657–1713): First king of Prussia.

5 Gottfried Wilhelm Leibnitz (1646–1716): German philosopher and mathematician.

by a pamphlet printed in Berlin in 1848, I do not dare to judge from the remote vantage point of the Vallon l'Ermitage. Below our garden the terrain drops away steeply; the far side of the valley is forested but we look across it at the lake; beyond the lake lies Fribourgian and Vaudian farmland, wooded hills rise all the way to the Alps, visible from the house on clear autumn and winter days or during the foehn,[6] from the Finsteraarhorn and the Blümlisalp all the way to Mont Blanc, even the Matterhorn discernible as a tiny spike, all the peaks part of the massif that shot up from the Tethys Sea a hundred million years ago in several mighty surges, the last of which thrust the Plateau Jura and the Chain Jura into the light. It is on the south slope of the latter that Neuchâtel and I have established ourselves. When I observe the several-million-year-older Alps and their foothills through the telescope, I can make out the church steeple of Guggisberg—my family comes from this village, and I am still a member of its 'citizens' community'[7]—the telescope I use for this is a large double-barrelled Zeiss on a tripod. Sometimes I use it to watch the Swiss air force at its target practice. About twenty kilometres away, near Estavayer, targets have been set up in the lake. Seen through the Zeiss they look like a town of stilt houses; the Mirages thunder past overhead and I can clearly distinguish the impacts. But mostly I use the Zeiss to observe the moon and the planets. Through it I can see Jupiter and Saturn crystal clear. When hunting spiral nebulas I employ a twenty-two-centimetre reflecting telescope which resembles a primitive

---

6 A warm, dry mountain wind.

7 In a tradition that is now losing importance, each Swiss citizen holds membership in a 'Bürgergemeinde' (citizens' community), generally inherited through the paternal line, independent of their birthplace or current residence.

canon, an unwieldy instrument which, when Sunday strollers stared over at me from the cliff with their binoculars, I elaborately set up and aimed at them—hastily the strollers abandoned their observation post. That was years ago. Now our garden is overgrown. When we moved into the house, the garden and the steep Alpine pasture adjoining it were free of trees to the cliff. Several fruit trees stood in the upper part of the garden, towards the cliff, cherries, plums and quinces, but the cherries and the plums were eaten by the birds; the forest was too near. Vegetable beds surrounded the house, edged by white Jura rocks. The beds looked like graves. The owner of the house had lived from his garden and tolerated no trees round the house, which was thus exposed to the blazing sun, a yellow cube with a flat roof (the first in Neuchâtel) which looked like a squashed hat. For two years the house had been unoccupied. It was too isolated for the Neuenburgers, said the owner who sold it, an attempt to reassure me, for somehow I suspected there was a different reason and as soon as we moved in the reason became apparent—the flat roof leaked. We called in an architect. He said the roof had to be renovated, at a cost one-tenth the price of the house. Having had to borrow even that from different sources, I was in no position now to have the roof renovated. Awaiting the deluges to come, I was sitting glumly in a cafe several weeks after the Munich premiere of *The Marriage of Mr Mississippi*,[8] when an old, massive man sat down across from me and immediately introduced himself. Judging by his name, he had to come from the same 'citizens' community' as I, and indeed he did come from Guggisberg; what is more, he had just come from Witzwil Prison and was enjoying his first hours of freedom in several months. In the course of the conversation I

[8] Play by Dürrenmatt, premiered in March 1952.

told him about my leaky roof, as the Guggisberger had once been a builder. Was there a door leading to the roof? he asked. I said there was. Did this door have an iron threshold? he asked next—by now we were on our second third-litre of Fendant—and I nodded again. Then he knew what the problem was, said the man from Witzwil. He'd repair the roof for me, it would cost me five francs. We drank the third third-litre of white wine, then he bought five francs worth of ship's putty at the Schneitter drugstore and we set out for the leaky house. He hammered away at the concrete beneath the iron threshold, used up the ship's putty, and the roof was leak-proof and stayed leak-proof until I had the house renovated thirteen years later. To this day I'm grateful to the man. Later we started planting trees, revamping the garden again and again, building a swimming pool and a studio, flowers replaced the vegetables, then shrubs and new trees replaced the flowers, and now, more than twenty-five years later, our garden has become part of the forest. But not only our garden is becoming overgrown, the valley is as well. Though the forest above our house, beyond the road, seems the same, the spruces, beeches and oaks that make up most of it have grown; climbing through, you find it less well-tended, wilder than it was; I make my way through it with difficulty. Private property. The forest beyond the cliff belongs to the municipality. My daily walks take me through it, accompanied over the past ten years by my two German shepherds, with whom I speak Bernese German. For the past three years it's been a new pair, but I haven't changed the names. The walk is always the same, a circuit, sometimes in the opposite direction. I like to develop ideas as I walk, barely noticing the forest; at one point there's still the rotting tree trunk I climbed over the first time holding the hand of my son who was not even five at the time. A forest changes only imperceptibly, but over the past three years it's been thinned out. It was as though the forest were slipping away from me. While before I walked through dense under-brush with my dogs, now the terrain emerged, revealing boulders I had never noticed before. Only now have I grown used to the thinning of the forest. But not only the forest has changed, Neuchâtel has as well, though this change dawned on me only gradually. Not for nothing did someone recently wonder why I never say 'Neuenburg'—if I could say 'Neuenburg', I would have accepted the city, but as 'Neuchâtel' I keep it at a polite distance; I have never felt fully at home. There are still neighbourhoods I don't know, as when a psychiatrist friend and I wandered down from the train station to his apartment, down stairs, through arcades I never knew were there, past an alcove chalked full with messages: 'Cherche fille, 15 ans, pour faire l'amour',[9] etc. And when I drive from the main post office towards the train station, I pass a little palace, hidden behind the houses on the left, which I've been meaning to take a look at for some time now, but it took me more than twenty years to notice it, and thus I still haven't looked at the little palace and prob-ably never will. As for the main post office on the harbour, it was the ugliest building in the city when we moved to Neuchâtel. The palatial edifice of yellow Neuenburg sand-stone, built sometime around the turn of the century, is suf-fused with the belief in the mission of the post office to bring nations together; beneath its gables, above the upper-most row of windows, the names of long-extinct states like Serbia and Montenegro are still engraved—here they have survived. Today, following its renovation, the post office is one of the city's most beautiful buildings, transfigured by the magic of nostalgia, a refreshing contrast to the modern building style whose inexorable march has not spared

9 'Seeking girl, fifteen years, to make love.'

Neuchâtel. From my theatre publisher's motorboat the town is no longer to be seen; it has become a suburb of the suburb Serrières, dominant with its high-rises. It's hard to make out where Neuchâtel lies; it almost takes an accident to discover the castle and the cathedral, and its Old Town is virtually buried. I occasionally show acquaintances the cathedral, the 'Collégiale'. The tomb of the last counts of Neuchâtel is not without its comical side. It used to be part of the floor, and the counts, once recumbent, now erected with the tomb slab and still praying in their suits of armour, have assumed a disconcertingly gay posture. In the castle, where the parliament met, my son, who refused to continue his military service, was sentenced to three months in prison on the grounds that his decision was not consistent with Kant's categorical imperative. When I asked the judge how he actually understood Kant's categorical imperative, he gave me a suspicious look and proclaimed that it was not his job to discuss the matter, Bern had decreed it. There are reasons why a carpet of stone covers the rest of Neuchâtel as well—as the city climbed the rocky ridge of the Chaumont, it dumped into lake what was pick-axed and shovelled out, causing the shore to close in on it. And a peculiarity of the city is that it turns its back on the lake. The lake teems with boats and sailing ships, but the banks, the high school, the art museum on its shore seem at night, unlit, like lifeless hulks. Neuchâtel is a city of walls. Not for nothing do its secret rulers include two building contractors whose families hail from Italy and Ticino. I often saw one of these secret rulers, now deceased, in Rocher, the pub belonging to my friend Liechti, that is, in the part of the pub that's a pub, not in the back room where it turns into a well-known restaurant. At first glance he seemed like a foreman from one of his many construction sites but he radiated a curious calm and assurance, the calm of the truly powerful—just as I imagine Ernst Jünger's Head Forester.[10] He greeted me courteously. My occasional digs about FC Xamax were shrugged off. This football club was an attempt by him and his clan to ingratiate themselves with the locals; the club plays a role in my life as well, since one of the few rudiments of Neuchâtel visible from our garden, apart from the roofs of three houses that loom above the trees on the opposite side of the valley and the steeple of the Catholic church down by the lake, is the football pitch; the mighty roar of the spectators resounds up to us when a goal is scored and deathly silence prevails when the club loses. Not only the football cheers reach us but also the noise of the city's celebrations—brass band music, drumming, the music from the stalls on the fairground by the post office, and sometimes, when I drive back from Zurich or Bern at night and see the people sitting in throngs outside the Escale or, across the way, the cafe Du Théâtre, I recall the time when I tried to feel at home in Neuchâtel. The attempt failed for a number of reasons: I never could particularly relate to French culture, and nothing that happened outside this culture counted in Neuchâtel. What was more, the writer Ludwig Hohl[11] lived with us for the first year. Not voluntarily—a well-known sculptor had called me from Geneva to tell me that Hohl was in the Bel-Air asylum and I had to get him out. It seemed that, whether in protest against the city or in protest against the humiliating circumstances in which he found himself, he had opened fire on a Geneva street, whereupon the police had committed him to the city asylum. I knew Hohl back from the years I spent on Lake Biel.

10 Reference to the dystopian novel *On the Marble Cliffs* (1939) by Ernst Jünger (1895–1998).

11 Ludwig Hohl (1904–80): Swiss literary outsider, discovered only late in life.

One night he'd called to tell me he was at the Kreuz inn. The cable railway was no longer running, so I walked down through the vineyards to the village and found Hohl at the Kreuz. But as soon as I'd greeted him we were arrested by two policemen. Trying to call me, Hohl had accidentally dialled the number of the Twann police station twice and, irritated, told them there was a murderer sitting in the Kreuz in Ligerz; only then had he managed to dial my number. I appeased the police with difficulty; I couldn't get round the fine but to my relief I was finally allowed to walk up with Hohl to the Festi[12] where I lived with my family. A full moon lit the vineyards almost bright as day, though in a blue-white light. I strode on ahead up the hill towards the Festi with Hohl a few yards behind me, constantly reciting in a loud voice: 'That you cannot end, that makes you great.'[13] Suddenly the Goethe quote sounded more muffled somehow. I turned round. Hohl was no longer to be seen. I walked down through the vineyards yelling 'Ludwig, Ludwig!' As though from the bowels of the earth came the muffled words: 'That you cannot end, that makes you great.' At last I found him; he had fallen into a sinkhole and I had trouble getting him out. In other respects as well, his stay in the Festi above Ligerz was not without its complications. He had a daughter by his ex-wife who lived in a children's home in a village in the Jura. Hohl developed highly complex plans to climb a mountain where he could observe his child through binoculars, calculated when he would have to set out, etc., but he never put his plans into action, sometimes mistrusting the weather, sometimes his binoculars. Then he returned to Geneva. The news that he had been committed

12 Artists' residence in the village of Ligerz.

13 Johann Wolfgang von Goethe, *The West-Eastern Divan* (John Whaley trans.) (London: Oswald Wolff, 1974), p. 35.

to the city asylum alarmed me. I travelled to Geneva. I found the well-known sculptor sitting fat and drunk in a pub between two equally fat, drunk whores, and the four of us set off by taxi to the asylum to rescue Hohl; with difficulty I managed to convince the whores not to accompany us into the asylum, as the drunk sculptor was baggage enough as it was. The senior physician didn't give us an overly friendly reception, especially once the sculptor lost his temper. In the end I was glad to be able to leave the asylum at all—without Hohl but with the cursing sculptor. Only a week later did I manage to get Hohl released. I went there without the sculptor. I had to promise to take Hohl to Neuchâtel. As soon as we left the asylum, he stopped the taxi and vanished. I was beginning to think he had bolted when he returned with two bottles of rum. He spent the journey to Neuchâtel sleeping in the luggage rack over me in the third-class compartment. It wasn't easy living with him. The children were still small, my mother-in-law was staying with us, the house was overcrowded. Hohl lived in a ground-floor room facing the path that led to the Rocher de l'Ermitage. He crisscrossed the room with strings where his aphorisms hung by clothespins, under which one moved as though beneath a spider's web. His work consisted not in rewriting his aphorisms but in rearranging them. In the mornings he worked and couldn't be disturbed; even a 'good morning' from my wife offended him. I worked at night, when he wanted to talk to me. We foundered on each other. Yelling his aphorisms out of the window, gesticulating wildly and reciting Rilke's 'Requiem' out loud in the forest beneath the cliff, he astonished and alarmed the people, mostly from the old-age home, who walked up the Vallon de l'Ermitage. The first summer we spent in Neuchâtel, the Neuchâtelers thought that Hohl was I and deplored my wife's misfortune to have ended up with such an eccentric husband. Hohl had trouble with my children too. He loved playing with them but did it with such intensity that they were afraid of him, now howling like a wolf, now roaring like a lion, only louder. I spent the afternoons using an iron bar to pry up the stones which my predecessor had spent his life setting in the ground to fence in his vegetables, and throw them out of the garden, where they rolled down the hill, delighting my children. Hohl often wanted to help me, for he had a passion for stones, which he considered more human than human beings. Laboriously he pried one of the stones from the ground, rolled it onto the grass, lay down beside it and fell asleep. The children stood in awe round Hohl and the stone. After about three months Hohl returned to Geneva. It was a liberation for him, as for us. On the last evening with us he acted out all the police encounters he anticipated on the Geneva streets after his return. He had an incomparable sense of comedy. His speedy arrest seemed inevitable. He was not arrested. Only in retrospect do I realize what bothered me about him: Hohl was an actor who had banished from his life the comedy that was natural to him. His poverty, his underground existence was a show. He aimed at tragedy. Thus his style: phrases that seem carved in marble, phrases claiming universal validity. He was a person I admired, whom I could offer no rejoinder but in whose sphere I was incapable of living. Who wants to be trapped in the Pyramid of Cheops? I had to get out into the open. But looking back it seems no accident that Neuchâtel confused me with Hohl. It confused something incomprehensible with something even more incomprehensible. For this city, a German-Swiss writer was in itself a thing of madness. Hohl lived up to this image more than I did—for them he was a German-Swiss *poète maudit*. I was too normal for them, especially once I started earning money. A woman who asked my children playing on the street what their father did, what his profession was, got the reply 'He tells stories.' The woman was puzzled. And rightly so. In Neuchâtel writing was something that teachers or otherwise serious people did as a sideline. That I was nothing but a writer was suspect. In Paris my plays were at best critical successes, not exactly flops, but at any rate such that when I went to buy bread after *Fous de Dieu* (*It is Written*, 1947) was performed in the Théâtre des Mathurins in Paris, the baker spontaneously slapped me on the back and exclaimed benevolently in Bernese German: 'Machet so wyter' (Keep it up). The first recognition I found in Neuchâtel. It was Yvonne Châtenay who first made me feel at home in the city. One day when I was leaving the Straussbrasserie on rue St-Honoré she approached me, at the time a woman of about fifty, with a pendulous lower lip and a Louis XVI face. Her movements were oddly slow. She said something about Wattenwil, a village at the foot of the Stockhorn near Thun. Not understanding what she meant, I shook the hand she offered me and replied that my mother was born in Wattenwil too. Then I took my leave. When I walked into Café Strauss a week later, the lady from Wattenwil asked me over to her regular table, in an alcove next to the door. I joined her. Evidently realizing that I still hadn't grasped who she was, she introduced herself for the second time: she was a von Wattenwyl by birth (Balzac mentions the family) married to a Neuenburger whom I met that evening as well. André looked the way one pictures a French aristocrat, his wife's ancient nobility had, as it were, rubbed off on him. Between the two World Wars they had led a grand life in Paris, and their fortune was gone by the time the war swept them back to Neuchâtel. He became the agent of an old wine dealer in Bordeaux who owned several castles and ate and drank nothing but Château d'Yquem and oysters; André always carried his wine list around with him in his bulging

wallet. He also framed engravings; I don't know what else
he dealt in. They lived in Auvernier in an old house, almost
a small castle, with a spiral staircase leading to the second
floor where they lived, having rented out the first floor. They
dwelt in three rooms filled with ancient furniture; the house
had belonged to André's father. Unfortunately, on the Wattenwyl side a painterly aunt had slipped in; her pictures
almost completely covered the walls. I would often tease
Yvonne about her background and she would say forcefully:
'Schwyg, Ungertan!' (Be silent, minion!). Along with music,
the two had another passion—football. Since they didn't
have a television, they came over to our place every time a
match was telecast. Then Yvonne would sit motionless in
front of the screen and every time the Swiss neared their
opponents' goal, she'd say: 'Schutt!' (Shoot!). Usually André
visited me by himself in the evening; we would drink a bottle of wine and listen to music without exchanging a word,
and then he would drive back down into town in his old Cit-
roën and pick up Yvonne, whom he had dropped off at Café
Strauss around noon. I know nothing for certain about
Yvonne's younger years. I believe I saw her once. I was about
seven when my parents hit upon the unfortunate idea of
teaching me the piano. They sent me to a piano teacher, the
daughter of the pastor of Oberdiessbach; it's hard for a pastor's son to escape his milieu. Every Saturday I had to go
down to the neighbouring village. The piano teacher held a
concert in the parsonage each year around Christmas where
she presented her pupils to their proud parents, including
two or three Wattenwyl girls, as I seem to recall, whether
from the nearby Oberdiessbach Castle or from somewhere
else, all considerably older than I but treated respectfully as
something extraordinary. To me they seemed incredibly
beautiful, noble and unapproachable. One of them may
have been Yvonne. I played 'On Horseback'; what Yvonne

played I don't know. Later Yvonne moved in high society with the natural assurance of a 'Watteville', went on great journeys, was friends with a maharaja. And then the sicknesses pounced on her like beasts, narcolepsy, Bang's disease, Parkinson's, she turned heavy, immobile, introverted, but she had the gift of drawing people to her. Through her I met Neuchâtel's originals, the sort of oddballs that only a small city can produce; a big one doesn't let them shine. The most striking thing about the group of regulars that formed at Yvonne's cafe table was that it mattered only that someone *was* something, not *what* he was. Thus one found the poor Russian émigré next to the government counsellor, a taciturn failed inventor next to the rector of the university, people I had no idea about next to literati and high-school teachers. The regular table was Yvonne's home, and gradually we felt a bit like 'Neuchâtelers', even if I knew that people made fun of my terrible French. But as it turned out, Yvonne would not be able to spend the rest of her life in Café Strauss; the building that housed the cafe was torn down to make way for one of the boring new buildings that now desolate the city of Neuchâtel. Café Strauss went down with flying colours, its death was like the death of old Neuchâtel. By mid-afternoon we had already gathered in the Strauss, determined to clean out the kitchen, storerooms and cellar to the very last. Now, it is futile to pretend that the memory of any given event has been preserved intact. What remains are details that overlap, lose their contours and get mixed up chronologically as well. What I recall of the death of this cafe, or rather of its dying, which drew on until the early morning hours, is an escalating bacchanal. It began as usual. We sat at Yvonne's table; contrary to his custom André was already there, that was the only unusual thing. The Russian émigré, the 'professional Russian', as I called him, was perhaps a touch more boisterous than he was otherwise, a high-school teacher from La Chaux-de-Fonds might, to celebrate the farewell, have imbibed more liquid courage than usual. Admittedly all this is still half-way reconstructable, and that I, otherwise a wine drinker, drank plum brandy because the cafe's owner provided the schnapps on the house is fairly certain. And so I drank in the wrong order from the beginning, probably everyone did—from the plum brandies, kirsch and marc we moved on to wine, first white, and Neuenburger at that, incidentally James Joyce's preferred beverage in the Kronenhalle.[14] Yvonne sat like a queen on her throne. André lamented the declining art of violin playing, excepting only Isaac Stern and perhaps Nathan Milstein. The forest and lake inspector founded a party with me—and that as the Bernese platter[15] was served, which in retrospect I find improbable, but everyone who took part in this farewell dinner, if still living, will recall a different menu. The goal of the party was to make the city of Neuchâtel into a small independent state on the model of Monte Carlo. We decided to give up La Chaux-de-Fonds, which would become the capital of the Canton of Jura, in turn to incorporate the Bernese Jura, a proposal which a separatist leader at the table categorically rejected, as meanwhile—we were drinking red now—the professional Russian forcefully demanded an appointment as Prince of Neuchâtel, being of nobility still older than the Romanovs, with Genghis Khan as one of his forefathers. His proposal fell flat. By now the first speeches were being held, cheese was served, it was time for the rarer wines. First the cafe owner was feted, then Yvonne. Then the mood turned patriotic—in a major speech the inspector defined Switzerland's three major governing parties, the Christians, the Liberals

14 A Zurich restaurant frequented by intellectuals.
15 A Bern speciality of mixed meats with sauerkraut.

and the Social Democrats, to the effect that the first believed in God, the fatherland and money, the second in the fatherland and money, and the third in nothing but money; the government counsellor gave a speech attacking the Vaudians who he claimed were nothing but Bernese pretending to speak French; the book dealer, a Vaudian, claimed that the express train from Neuchâtel to Lausanne had recently derailed when it ran over a grape just past Neuchâtel. Then, over sausages, the professional Russian began to vent the ire he'd been nursing for years against Neuchâtel, where he led a life of squalor. His tirade had a relentless force; he presented the Neuenburgers with a list of all their faults, summed up their sins, exponentiated their vices; his Russian soul brimmed over, gushed past Neuchâtel, poured out over Switzerland, this monstrous den of philistines that had produced such wretched pigmies as the heretic Calvin and the blasphemous Zwingli. But rather than growing angry the Neuenburgers egged him on, clapping and shouting bravo the more the professional Russian frothed at the mouth. The whole restaurant was packed, from my seat I couldn't tell what was going on at the other tables, suddenly champagne was served, everyone was roaring drunk, including the police. The party I had founded with the forest and lake inspector split into me and him, he wanted to found a second Vatican in Neuchâtel, which I condemned as politically unrealistic; my translator held a speech against French music; the rector of the university addressed me as 'notre Aristophanes' while I called him 'mon cher Hérodot', a form of address which we later retained; a quiet German-Swiss bank clerk who never said a word, but for some reason had won Yvonne's favour, demanded to sleep with the waitress on the spot, under the table; the high-school teacher from La Chaux-de-Fonds, a Jew, held a speech in the style of a local federal counsellor; and all struck up the national anthem. I hardly remember a thing about the cafe's end, only, vaguely, a groping search in the emptied cellar to see if there were any more bottles left, and then early in the morning the arrival of the workers who began with the demolition. The tables and chairs were transported away, Café Strauss was dead. A new meeting place was sought and found in the Café Du Théâtre, but it wasn't the same any more—people rarely dropped by Yvonne's table, the food was mediocre. Yvonne's group of regulars became a sadder and sadder sight, many died, she admitted people she never would have admitted before. She was confined more and more to her bed and as in any case the Neuchâtelers' passion is bridge, her table was often abandoned, only the new rector of the university, a theologian, sat and played chess with the head of the Jewish community—Ormuzd and Ahriman, though I didn't know which of the two was Ormuzd and which Ahriman. When I think back on this time, I realize the extent to which I was forced back into my interior space—writing becomes more difficult with the accumulation of things experienced, repressed and not experienced. No doubt this explains my difficulties with Neuchâtel—my work has thrust itself more and more inexorably between me and the city. I no longer notice it. Not from disdain but from self-protection. And not only the city. Visitors often ask me how I manage to write with the nine larger-than-life figures of the 'Salvation Army' by Varlin,[16] with this huge painting in my study, how can I stand to see them as I write (now they're hanging in my studio)? And who doesn't admire our view? I am aware of it rarely, for moments, all at once. In the summer evenings cows trotted along the meadow past my garden, coming from the farm at the

16 Willi Guggenheim aka Varlin (1900–77): Swiss painter and close friend of Dürrenmatt.

bottom of the valley. At night their bells tinkled, now near, now far, and two years ago early one morning they made their way in through the open garden gate. The dogs ran wild, barking, and chased off all the cows but one. When I came down the huge animal was standing helplessly half in the kitchen, gaping at me, then fled into the pergola, but then, instead of taking the path through the still-open garden gate, it stood mooing hollowly, having broken halfway through the porch roof over the doghouse. I called the farmer who came with his tractor and stared at the cow in astonishment, he'd never seen anything like it; then he freed the beast from its plight. It was summer, five in the morning. I strolled through the cow-free garden, gazed down the Vallon, the lake blazed up like a vast mirror, I saw it all as though for the first time, I was in a wide-open space, no longer in the labyrinths and caves of my youth, where the Emmental enclosed me with its fir woods. This year the cows stayed away, the nights are even quieter than usual, now and then an aeroplane, noise from the train station only towards morning. The Vallon changes imperceptibly—earlier I could watch the football games on the Maladière through my telescope, now the trees down on rue Matile and in my garden have grown too tall; the Catholic church from the end of the last century has long since lost its English-seeming pseudo-Gothic touch, the crenulations of its red tower having fallen victim to an architect who tried to modernize it, and now the tower is truly ugly. Mitigating nostalgia refuses to materialize; that will take another century. But from our house the town itself is hidden from me not only by the forested side of the valley over which I see the lake but above all by myself, since I moved here so that I would not have to participate in any cultural life whatsoever. I make my own culture and am just as reluctant to go to the theatre in Neuchâtel as in Zurich or Munich. I don't like going to the theatre at all. But there are always social pressures, and so I sought refuge from German-Swiss culture in Neuchâtel. Not that I am completely free here. The theatre next to the town hall is small and dilapidated—and I was glad that it used to feature the Gala Kersenty, which no one expected me to attend—but, for example, when the Théâtre de l'Est visited from Strasbourg with *Romulus* (1950) and *The Visit* (1956), my presence was imperative and I sat there on tenterhooks, quasi as a cultural representative, though the productions, directed by Gignoux,[17] were outstanding. It does not reflect badly on the city, though, that plans for a new theatre have not yet been realized. It's better to have no theatrical life than the mediocre, highly subsidized kind that is cultivated in German Switzerland. The times have driven theatre from the stage. But it is not my doing that the natural order of the Vallon de l'Ermitage has been maintained for so many years. I owe it to my neighbour, the notary, an old bachelor who lives in an old villa about two hundred yards below me, before the valley begins its upward slope. Only recently did we begin greeting each other again when, sitting as far away from each other as possible, we eat at the Rocher. I greet him with a polite nod, he greets me with pathos, exaggerated politeness—an old man with character. Along with the steeply sloping meadow that runs beneath my garden and the cliff he owns nearly the entire Vallon along with its ramshackle farms whose occupants groan beneath his whims as the farmers once groaned beneath the bailiffs—the current farmer must be the fourth we've known. The first time I visited the maître in his office in town to purchase my current house with the money I had borrowed, he regarded me with suspicion. Though merely the owner's notary, he was in fact the crucial person. No one

---

17 Hubert Gignoux (1915–2008): French actor and theatre director.

in town dared to contradict him, least of all the old city engineer who wanted to sell me the house. I saw my chances dwindling away. The maître's suspicion was not unfounded. My appearance was dubious. I wore a long coat that was much too baggy for me, a present from a concert singer for whom it had also grown too baggy. The maître was put off. But a distant approval glimmered in his sceptical gaze when I assured him, on being asked, that we didn't have a dog— previously he'd had a man who wanted to buy the house and turn it into a dog home, and the maître, who hated dogs, prevented the purchase. Thanks to my doglessness, he offered me no legal resistance. A certain friendly neighbourliness began to develop, albeit with Neuenburg's interpersonal chill; like many in the canton, the maître was originally from Bern. We visited him once and once he visited us. We ate by candlelight in the 'built-in' library. Then an old colonel we knew from Bern gave us his old dog. The amiable patrician was reluctant to part with the animal but it gave him allergies, and we couldn't resist his pleas. It was a cocker spaniel, a dog so doggish he drove you crazy. He followed me round, inseparable. Inadvertently I shut doors in his face, a constant whining filled the house, he barked in the garden. The maître saw this dog as a breach of loyalty. His barking got on my nerves too, I admit. Unfortunately, the maître launched his war against our dog by registered post, sending us letter after letter instead of persuading me, over a bottle of good wine, to give the dog to another dog lover, especially given that I wasn't really a dog lover in the first place—his registered letters made me into one. And I was careless enough to talk about the dog war between the maître and me in Café Strauss and when asked how I had replied to him, I fibbed—more from embarrassment due to the fact that I never answer letters than from cockiness— saying I'd written the maître that I had read his letters to my dog in the hope that the animal would take them to heart. My fib ended up in the newspapers and relations with my neighbour deteriorated. We stopped greeting each other. The cocker spaniel lived to a ripe old age. He coexisted with the cats we had back then. First it was just one, brought with us from the Festi, but she had as many as sixteen kittens a year. I gave the first eight to the farmer down the valley to kill. He gave me a look and took the animals without a word. In that instant I realized I was a coward in his eyes— if you keep cats, you must also be able to kill them. The farmer took the kittens away. From then on I killed the kittens myself. I examined them, left the mother a tomcat and carried the others into the orchard, dug a hole, threw them in, shovelled dirt over them, trod it down, six years long, I'd killed more than eighty kittens, I felt like a cat Eichmann. Our house teemed with tomcats, the mother cat had litter after litter. When her time would come, she'd slink round me, purring, and finally sit on my typewriter. Then I knew what I had to do. I would fix up a box for her, filled with rags, set milk at the ready, she would begin to bring forth young and I would begin to kill. Then came the great cat extinction. A doctor in the south of France released a bacillus. His target was the rabbits that were ravaging his garden, and they stopped ravaging it after that, but the doctor unleashed an epidemic—the bacilli also attacked cats. Not just the French cats but ours as well. The borders offered no protection. First the tomcats were crippled, crawling about the house and crying piteously. They succumbed three days later. All this dying went on for two weeks. Only the mother was left alive. I had her sterilized. After that she changed, began to stray, finally never came back. The cocker spaniel was left by himself, blind, his sense of smell declining too. He preferred to stay in the kitchen. We bought a Bernese mountain dog from a farmer in the Jura, a huge beast. But the way the farmer treated the Bernese mountain dog should have made me suspicious; he treated him like a dog, beating him brutally, kicking him. Buddy was fearful and later turned dangerous. We had built him a kennel. The first day he ran wild in it; gradually he got used to us but it was too much for the maître. He filed a lawsuit with the city council, claiming that I had erected a building right on the boundary between the two properties, his and mine. The city council responded that this building consisted only of a wall and an Eternit roof, the doghouse beneath it could not be described as a building. My neighbour's rancour increased. The Bernese mountain dog was not to be restrained, from the roof of the kennel he easily gained the street. Now and then he trotted into the city and lay down outside someone's front door. We got phone calls from people who didn't dare to leave the house. I brought the dog back home with difficulty. Then the beast ensconced itself behind the maître's hedge, the children called me, strollers and little children were staring through the hedge at the nearly St Bernard–sized mountain dog and the maître stood rigid with anger in the garden. I tried to lead the dog away through the hedge but the hedge was impenetrable, I had no choice but to go the long way round via the farmhouse at the bottom of the valley. But the maître told me gruffly to use the path through his garden. I hesitated, my children were agog: What would Papa do? The giant dog trembled with fear, for his sake I obeyed the maître, went through his garden, dragged the dog out from behind the hedge, walked back through the garden with him. The maître was victorious and in the flush of his victory greeted me in flawless German. I shook his hand, ashamed of my 'lack of character', and resolved to ignore him from then on, and so we ignored each other. The maître's fate, mine, and that of the Bernese mountain dog took their course. All three of us remained true to our principles, all three of us being Bernese by origin. The mountain dog gradually developed into a wild beast that guarded us fanatically. When my father took a walk, Buddy wouldn't let him back into the garden; a director who was staying with us went swimming in the pool between the upper and lower houses early one morning and Buddy refused to let him out of the water, so that the half-frozen man of the theatre had to be rescued by the maidservant; then he began to attack people, starting with a Danish journalist. First I hadn't wanted to receive the man, then agreed to half an hour—after I'd taken him to the hospital, he had to spend three days with us. Then he bit a sculptor, then a teacher who entered the garden despite my warnings—he claimed to know how to deal with Bernese mountain dogs—then a friend of my son, then the sculptor again, after that the two daughters of our auto mechanic—when they picked up our car for an overhaul the creature must have seen it as theft—he also bit the beekeeper, and finally he bit the gamekeeper, they spent four hours stitching him in the hospital. Despite my wife's pleas there was no other choice, I had to do what I should have done long before. It was Christmas, the candles on the tree were lit, I took the Bernese mountain dog to the veterinarian who had placed the creature with us in the first place. The dog followed me willingly, he loved sitting in the back of the car. Even at the vet he suspected nothing, he licked my hand as the vet gave him the injection, then laid himself down, slowly and tidily, as he always did, as though he were going to sleep. 'When will he be dead?' I asked. 'Now,' replied the vet. But his death affected us less deeply than that of the little tricolour papillon who was run over a few yards below our house. The butterfly dog was a sort of miniature fox with enormous bat ears and a sweeping tail that trailed on his back in a cascade of white hairs. If ever I truly loved a dog, it was him, though actually he kept me at a distance. Only during thunder-storms did the little dog press up to me and scratch at me impatiently, no doubt expecting me to be able to switch off the thunder. In 1969, my wife travelled to the US with my daughter and my sister. I had the first year of Basel under my belt.[18] *King John* had premiered, later *Play Strindberg*; I was on edge, full of plans, eager to work. Aware that I was neglecting my family, I wanted them to have some fun—a trip to America would do them good. Now they were gone, Easter came, Easter Monday, the maid had the day off, my mother was visiting from Bern. On Tuesday evening I sat in the study with my son, discussing theology. Just as my father had once tried to persuade me to become a pastor, I now tried to persuade my son not to become one. Both attempts failed. Around one in the morning I went down to the lower house, accompanied by the dog. I was tired. I undressed. On the toilet the pain started. At first I thought it was heartburn, took Ebimar, went to bed, the dog cuddled against my neck, his warmth did me good, though the pain grew more severe. I got up, went down to the library, got down *The Turning Point* by Klaus Mann—a book that once had bored me—to check a passage which Peter Bichsel[19] had men-tioned a few days before. The dog followed me. Back in my bedroom I lay down again. The dog cuddled up to me. The pain grew more intense. I tried to distract myself by reading but the book left me cold. I was annoyed that I hadn't taken a different book, and yet didn't have the strength to fetch a different one. My belly was distended. I kept going to the bathroom and sitting on the toilet. The dog followed me anxiously. Then I lay down in bed again, the pain piercing

18 From 1968 to 69 Dürrenmatt served as an advisor to the director of the Basel Theatre.

19 Peter Bichsel (1935–): Swiss writer and columnist.

from the middle of my chest to under my chin, my left armpit aching, my left arm and left hand tingling. The dog slid up as though it didn't want to weigh on my left shoulder. I knew I was having a heart attack but went on calmly reading the book that meant nothing to me—I might as well have been reading the phone book—the dog's little head nestled against my cheek. Sometimes I paced up and down in the bedroom, the pain filling me so implacably it was as though I had to concentrate on it to stay alive. I was completely indifferent, barely noticing the little dog which sat in the middle of the room when I paced up and down. It didn't occur to me to wake up my mother, sleeping in the next room, I had forgotten her. Neither did I call my son in the upper house, I had forgotten him too. It simply didn't cross my mind. The only sad thing was that I wouldn't see my wife again, though I was too apathetic to be sad. It occurred to me that parting words would sound best in French. Then I reached for the book again, somewhat bewildered at what was evidently the last book I'd ever read—what did Klaus Mann mean to me?—realized that Bichsel had been mistaken and went on reading mechanically anyway, to still the pain. Dying was something I'd pictured differently. Around six-thirty I fell asleep, at seven-thirty I woke up. It was the painlessness that woke me. The dog lay curled up beside me. I stretched happily—a false alarm. Just as I was flooded by an indescribable feeling of health, the pain descended upon me with full force. It was as though a knife were lacerating my chest, but that was when I was galvanized into action, perhaps because there was no defence against this pain. I picked up the phone book, tried to find a doctor, I had a name in mind but had forgotten it. I phoned my son and told him to take me to a doctor, any doctor. I dressed and went down the stairs, the dog accompanying me. The maid, back from her vacation, stared at me fearfully. I was sick, I yelled at her—senselessly—and where was my son? He was already waiting in the car and drove me into town. It hadn't been easy to find a doctor, most were still on vacation, but then suddenly I was lying on the examination couch—electrocardiogram, blood sample, much palpating and pressing of my abdomen, at last the diagnosis: gastritis. But that wasn't the alarming thing: my liver was swollen, my blood sugar at six hundred, a sanatorium stay was urgently advised. The only healthy organ was my heart. I was seized by a wild joy. The pain hadn't let up yet but the doctor gave me a prescription and I immediately bought two bottles of a milky liquid, Maloxon, I'd handle the blood sugar somehow. At home I went to bed, relieved. The dog snuggled up to me again. The pain remained. I drank a whole bottle of the milky liquid, couldn't sleep. In the evening I went to the upper house to distract myself by watching *The Avengers* on television. It was an effort to walk uphill. I returned to the lower house with the dog. Starting the second bottle of Maloxon, I tried to chat with my mother who was in a good mood; all I had was a harmless attack of indigestion. The little dog lay on my lap while my mother talked about my grandmother's death, laughing as she told the story—aged three, I had come to her worried that grandmother wouldn't go to Heaven, she was so fat she was sure to get stuck in the chimney. As she chatted away, I thought about Varlin and how he'd painted me with the little dog on my lap, barely listening to my mother. I went to bed with the dog, took Valium and Peroben, the pain subsided, just a slight burning now and then, I fell asleep, the dog snuggled up to me. The next day I woke without pain and lay in bed until close to noon. At lunch I was so weak I could hardly lift the spoon. Now I did begin to wonder. I tried to call my doctor in Bern, he was on vacation with his family, the hospital refused to give me his address, suddenly

I knew where to reach him. It was like an inspiration; that evening I had him on the phone. He said my son should drive me to his office in Bern the next day. My son drove me, I didn't take anything with me, still convinced of the Neuenburg doctor's diagnosis, the only thing I feared was an increase in my daily dose of insulin. The doctor, a long-time friend, examined me, first taking my blood pressure, fell silent, which wasn't like him, took a blood sample, gave it to his lab technician, prepared the cardiogram, still silent, then cut the cardiogram into sections, laid the sections on a commode, contemplated them, said: 'Come here.' I stood up, went over to him, stared uncomprehendingly at the cardiogram, asked: 'Well?' 'Heart attack,' he replied. But the blood sugar was fine. The diagnosis was a shock. The doctor acted with sangfroid—if I'd survived for three days now, I might as well come over to his house for lunch. I ate little. Afterwards my doctor went into town with me. He acted unconcerned but I could feel him watching me. We went into a bookshop. 'Pick out enough books for six weeks,' he told me dryly. I chose Fischer's *History of the World* in thirty volumes and then we took a taxi to the hospital. I felt wretched and forlorn. In the meantime my son had already driven to Neuchâtel and come back with the necessities, including several volumes of Marcel Proust whom I hadn't yet managed to finish. Later he also brought a crate with the best wines from my cellar. The first night was troubled, the doctor was called to my bedside again. Though no one knew where my wife and daughter were in the US, they were with me two days later. By chance my wife had visited the Swissair office in Chicago and, learning of my illness, called my doctor; all the preparations for their return flight had already been made. The long weeks in the hospital began, a dogged struggle to regain my mobility, disastrous visits by writers who failed to grasp that in my state I had no interest in them, in their writing or mine, that I kept myself busy out of sheer self-protection so that I wouldn't have to cope with them on top of it all. I started Fischer's *History of the World* with Volume 16, *Central Asia*; it seemed best to read something as exotic as possible. Proust proved to be unsuitable reading material; I read my way into a veritable animosity against the I that claims to be Proust. Finally, once I had returned to Neuchâtel, my wife drove me to Schuls in the Lower Engadine. It was June, with snow flurries in the Vorarlberg. The hotel was located in the middle of the village. I regained my footing with an effort. News of the difficulties which the Basel Theatre was creating for itself began to reach Schuls. Frisch, who had already visited me in Bern, was staying in Tarasp. In his *Diary* he recorded the last evening we spent together: 'It's not true that he's incapable of listening. When the innkeeper in Schuls sits down at our table and has stories to tell (e.g. how someone like Aga Khan gets fleeced in the Grisons), but then ends up just yakking away, Friedrich Dürrenmatt is a Hercules of a listener; it depends on the interlocutor.' A pity that Frisch didn't listen as well. I've forgotten the story about Aga Khan but not what the innkeeper told me about the Lower Engadiners in Schuls—for example, about a carpenter who the innkeeper had thought was the only one who spoke nothing but Romansh[20] and didn't understand German. He found him one morning standing on a stool and pressing his palms against a section of the ceiling. The innkeeper asked in Romansh what the carpenter was doing. He lowered his hands from the ceiling, looked up and said in German: 'May God permit it stick a bit.' Then, climbing down from the chair and glancing back up at the ceiling, he added: 'And God permitted it sticked a bitted.' After that evening I would not

20 A Rhaeto-Romance language spoken in the canton of Grisons.

see Frisch for eight years, we next met at Varlin's funeral. In July my wife and I returned to Neuchâtel. It must have been some time that summer that André visited me again, again we listened to music, my wife laughed at our silence. He died soon after. I have only a confused, contradictory recollection of the circumstances. He called to tell me that he had been in Barcelona, in the Ritz, and had a dizzy spell, whereupon he discovered champagne, which had healed him, he had often felt a pressure on his chest but the champagne took this pressure away. I sensed I was hearing his voice for the last time. Yvonne was put in an old-age home in Bern. I hardly went to the forsaken cafe table any more, usually there were strangers sitting there. And so we were left with no one but the maître. Once he'd sent an indecipherable letter, perhaps I didn't want to decipher it. Once I'd seen him in Venice, we walked past each other. He's a character, I'm a character—thus over nearly thirty years, from sheer character, we lost out on each other. I admit that the calculus works to my advantage: I owe him much, he owes me nothing. Grasping that your life is where you live and hoping to give his life, transient like every life, a certain semblance of permanence, he left the Vallon de l'Ermitage untouched and sold no land for building. It remains the valley for the old people from the home at its entrance, for Sunday strollers and lovers. I have purchased the steeply sloping meadow below my houses to forestall speculators. But time is mightier than man and his intentions. Already I've had to fell several trees I planted. Though the city developed along the lake and towards the Chaumont above the canton hospital, changes loomed for the Vallon as well. The city has grandiose plans: not only does it want highway access, like every Swiss locality, it also wants the highway to pass through town; why they do so is unclear. Towards Biel the plain between Lake Neuchâtel and Lake Biel has already been disfigured by a highway which is ultimately pointless, since it joins a smaller road in the canton of Bern. It is as though Neuchâtel, whose charm is that it has missed the present, refuses to miss the future. But to be fair, it was only the redoubled disfigurement of a disfigured region. Years before, the Cressier Refinery was built on the plain between the two lakes with that sixth sense that characterizes the Swiss in general—the sense for building the most dangerous things in the most dangerous places. Depending on the water level, the canal between Lake Neuchâtel and Lake Biel also flows into Lake Murten, or the other way round; finally, after some back and forth, everything flows into the Aar. Cressier is one of the many ticking Swiss time bombs. Now the highway, which already passes the refinery, is interrupted at St Blaise, beginning again only past Neuchâtel. In the hopes of reaching Yverdon, even Lausanne one day ten years from now, you can race along it almost as far as Boudry, about twelve kilometres, where it suddenly comes to an end with ostentatious exits leading to the wine villages and placing them, as it were, under quarantine. Evidently the city stands in the way of the project. For the ten minutes required to cross it at rush hour, twice a day, the decision was made to tunnel under it. This will make the city vanish, so to speak, when already, every time I'm abroad, I have to explain elaborately where Neuchâtel is. Soon strangers will zoom along under Neuchâtel and past its shores without noticing the city. The planners proceeded with care. First they filled in the shoreline under the pretext of building the highway there, certain that the population would put up a fight. It put up a fight. The resulting expanse of asphalt serves as a parking area, intruding between the city and the lake. Then the Federal Council in Bern was allowed to decide for the tunnel which the planners in Neuchâtel wanted. If anything can be planned at all, it is by our supreme authorities—which are already in the process of transforming the nation of herdsmen into a nation of moles. Trusting in their functionality, the terrain was explored, there was drilling everywhere, and as a highway tunnel needs a flue to conduct away the exhaust, this flue was planned in the forest near my house, above the Vallon de l'Ermitage. The little valley is popular though. A committee was formed against the exhaust flue and one day we gathered on the cliff, about fifty men. The weather was inclement, rainy and cold. We stood on the Rocher de l'Ermitage, at our feet my property, the valley, the city, the lake above which the rain clouds roiled. The city engineer and the representative of the Zurich firm which was to build the tunnel explained their plan. A little flag fluttered above my home, seemingly deep in the forest. Rainy as it was, said the city engineer, you couldn't ask anyone to walk all the way over there, that was why he'd organized the meeting on the cliff, here was the best view, the flag was visible, everyone could satisfy themselves that the site was remote and would bother no one. But the group refused to be deterred, now that we'd gathered, we wanted to inspect the site of the flue. The city engineer was forced to give in. We climbed down the stone steps that lead up the cliff and walked along a narrow forest path to the site where the flue was planned. We stood in a small clearing in the middle of which the pole with the flag had been erected. Round the flag were little bushes and shrubs, next to each plant a brown-painted stake whose slanted end bore a green sign with the botanical name of the bush or shrub. Two men in tracksuits, one blue and one white, came running along the forest path, joggers, the path was part of a fitness trail. Suddenly the city engineer was uncertain, said no final decision had been made on the flue or on its site, it would take weeks before its site could be determined but it had to be possible to present the road-tunnel project to the public. A notary interjected that the road-tunnel project included the exhaust-flue project, and if both these projects weren't presented to the public at the same time, it would be possible to build the flue without a public hearing. Didn't the notary trust the authorities? asked the city engineer. The notary replied that he mistrusted all authorities on principle and a geology professor suggested building the exhaust flue at the Carrière de Tête *plumée*. He was the only one who knew anything about this quarry. There were many of them on the south slope of the Chaumont, where the Jura stone is extracted. Once a quarry reaches a certain size, it is abandoned. This quarry, ten minutes from my house, is abandoned as well. One of the secret rulers stores his enormous machines there. Now everyone wanted to see the Carrière de Tête *plumée*. It was right nearby, said the professor, you could reach it by car. That wasn't necessary, it was barely five hundred yards above my house, in the forest. I had simply never noticed it as it's reached by a poorly asphalted road and I hate tarred roads when I walk in the forest with my dogs, I like to feel the forest floor. The cavalcade halted. I steered my car onto a side path and, with my lawyer, followed the men who were now continuing up the road on foot. To keep it from becoming too steep, a wall had been built, over which the asphalted road passed like a sort of ramp. Past the wall the road conformed to the sloping terrain again. The cavalcade had halted anyway due to the fact that past the wall the road was barred by an iron pole. Next to this barrier stood a dilapidated shack. The iron pole could be raised only by means of a key, which meant that the truck drivers—whether they didn't have the key or had forgotten it or were too lazy to drive any further—had dumped their waste over the wall into the forest and now the wall itself was nearly invisible beneath this unsightly waste. We walked round the barrier, which kept only the cars from proceeding further, followed the road which hardly deserved the name now, black and sloppily tarred as though tar had flowed down from above, to our left the forest, dead wood, ivy-smothered trees, to our right heaps of yellow Neuenburg stone, and between them, over and over again, tar, asphalt slabs, plastic, scrap metal, helter-skelter, ahead of us, on the horizon we climbed towards, solitary larches against the cloudy, rain-soaked sky. Then we were at the top and found ourselves at the edge of a crater, an impression caused by the fact that the southern end of the quarry which had been cut out of the ridge was closed off by a mound of earth. Having climbed up from the west, we were standing where the mound merged back into the natural terrain. Opposite us was the eastern wall of the quarry, bare Jura rock, white limestone in parallel layers, tilted like the mountain ridge, resembling thick, greyed, stacked-up carpets, the north side of the quarry was also bare Jura rock and on a concrete ramp built over it stood an orange monster of a tanker surrounded by waste workers in orange protective suits. From the tanker a mighty black jet of filth shot over the concrete ramp and the whitish Jura rock into the centre of the crater at our feet. It was like a dinosaur with diarrhoea—the shit splattered down into a black oily lake scattered with plastic bottles. A strange solemnity settled over the men. All were embarrassed by the sight. The quarry was Neuchâtel's cesspit. The dump—no patriotism goes untouched by such places. What the road workers pumped from the sewers or the gullies ended up in this vast, indecent hole, probably also the sludge from the sewage-treatment plant and in earlier times the heating oil residues which hadn't yet seeped away. This dark swill leaked slowly through the layers of rock on which, lower down, my house and studio stood, eating its way towards the lake on whose stony slopes and filled-in shores the city lay. We went home in silence. Once, when I returned later, a cloud of huge black birds rose, crows, a smell of blood hung over the dump. It stank of murder. I tossed a stone into the blackish sludge, it sank slowly, sending up bubbles, a sluggish eddy formed, turning red. From the edge of the dump you could see far down the lake towards Yverdon—a more idyllically located dump is hard to picture. And if I visit this place again and again and show it to my friends, it is only because it evokes memories of the village where I grew up. As children we often played in its rubbish pit, the rusty spokes, corroded milk cans, broken sewing machines, etc., were transformed into fantastical toys, and in the evening I loved to ride my father's bike there as the sun set, past the old cemetery, over the bridge, past the new cemetery; as yet there were no houses there, a dirt track led across the plain to the rubbish pit; I pictured myself gliding in a ship across an immeasurable ocean, talked out loud to myself, rode back and up to the pit again until the first stars could be seen, and then I rode home. And as I stood there for the first time at the edge of that forsaken crater filled with that vile slurry of faeces and sewage sludge, sunk into the forest above the place where I live and work, only then did I realize, a quarter-century after ending up in this region, on this lake and above this city, where I actually live. And I realized more than that—the actor Hans Christian Blech once told me that, in the Second World War, during the German advance into Russia, he had been assigned to a penal company. Late one afternoon, having advanced into vacant territory, without supplies, he went off by himself in the gathering dusk to find food. A farmer pointed him to a forest where he found a clearing filled with chanterelles, more mushrooms than he'd ever seen before; laden with chanterelles he returned to the penal company. Two years later, as the German army was retreating, he found himself near this forest at the same time of year and set out again to find the clearing but the clearing was fenced in, and over the gate stood 'Katyn', the name of the forest in which Stalin had thousands of Polish officers murdered. He always thought of that, said the actor, when he played Woyzeck and came to the place where he has to say to the doctor: 'It's the mushrooms, Doctor. It's all in the mushrooms. Have you noticed the patterns they make on the ground? If only we knew how to read what they say.'[21] Now we can read these patterns—through the associations they evoke. My village's rubbish pit could be transformed by children into a playground, the enormous dump above the Vallon de l'Ermitage cannot. The rubbish pits of my youth are not what they are today. These are signs that evoke other associations, images of murderous deeds, visions of dumps for human beings, such as Auschwitz. The mushrooms' patterns have become the patterns people will leave behind on the earth—atomic waste dumps as the sole testimony that man the rapacious ape once existed. Only once they have decayed will the planet, the gift that brought us forth, be pristine once again.

Postscript '81: The winter did not agree with me, nor with the new German shepherds. The snow came too early, lingered, iced over. The deer came down through the forest even at the hour I took my walks, the male dog—we've had him for three years—had to be leashed, the female dog—the same age as the male, we've had her a few weeks longer—I let run free: she's too playful to be a danger to the deer. The police saw things differently. I stopped taking walks. They were too much trouble what with the ice and the agitated dog on the leash. And so I was not in a very

21 Georg Büchner, *Complete Plays, Lenz, and Other Writings* (John Reddick trans.) (London: Penguin, 1993), p. 122.

good mood on my sixtieth birthday and it embarrassed me to be celebrated by Neuchâtel, but suddenly I sensed that I'd become a Neuenburger—you can't spend half your life in a city with impunity. Five days later in Zurich, for whose theatre I had written and worked and where most of my friends live, I certainly didn't feel like a Zuricher. I never felt like one, nor like a city-Berner, nor like a Basler, and the theatre was guarded by police, the 'youth' had formed ranks outside, as the mayor and the president of the state were present. And so I was celebrated behind closed doors, under quarantine. While the Zurich events were official, those in Neuchâtel were familial. Not only did the grandson of the pastor to whose vacation home in La Tourne I had ridden my bike more than forty years ago, passing through Neuchâtel for the first time, play Bach's Chromatic Fantasy and Fugue to start with, the Konolfingen Yodel Choir, so taken for granted, suddenly fit me better than the performance of *Romulus* in Zurich. As the young pianist played, I thought of how I had seen his grandfather for the last time: he had moved from Rochefort to Zurich and lay dying in a bare ground-floor room facing the street in some spooky little hospital. And the Konolfingers made me wonder if one of them had been one of those strapping farm boys who had trounced me back then and could trounce me so because they were older than I, and then I realized that I was now older than most by far of the yodellers with their pale beige costumes and their flat black hats and that only a few could be almost or just as old as I. When the auditorium of the Cité universitaire, where the festivities were held, had gradually emptied, in the last row I noticed an old man without recognizing him, so greatly had he changed. It was the maître. I went over to him. 'Je suis un encore là,'[22] he said.

---

22 'I am still there.' (Incorrect French.)

Later I went up to the city with the rector and a few acquaintances. The authorities had had Liechti prepare a meal in the Rocher. I was accompanied by my doctor from Bern, we climbed a seemingly endless flight of stairs towards the train station, I sensed in him the same concern about me as then, when he accompanied me to the bookshop to pick out my reading material for my hospital stay. At Liechti's, where the others had already gathered, I met the maître again. He had been invited on my request but insisted that the city had invited him. 'Nous payerons quand-même,'[23] he declared. Then he stayed until nearly eleven. A friend of Liechti's, an innkeeper at whose inn I sometimes eat, brought him home. I said goodbye: 'Au revoir, Maître.' And he said: 'Le Maître, c'est vous, car je ne suis qu'un centimètre.'[24] It was his first understatement. Once the innkeeper had taken him home, the maître ordered him to come inside. The innkeeper, an amiable German-Swiss, obeyed. The maître sat down in an armchair in his vestibule, put his feet on another chair, and ordered: 'Enlevez-moi les chaussures!'[25]

23 'We will pay all the same.'

24 'You are the master, as I am only a centimetre.'

25 'Take off my shoes.'

My drawings are not a sideline to my literary works; they are the battlefields, sketched and painted, on which my writerly struggles, adventures, experiments and defeats take place—a realization which first came to me while leafing through this book, although in my youth I only drew and did not begin writing until later on. I was always a draughtsman. But *Crucifixion I* is the first drawing of mine which I still find acceptable, for the simple reason that I am a 'dramaturgical' draughtsman, not a compositional one. I am concerned not with the beauty of the image but with its possibilities. To cite an example from 'great' art—Michelangelo's *David* is an absurdity, a colossus, 5.5 metres tall, when according to the Bible Goliath stood only 2.9 metres. But *David* is a great piece of sculpture because Michelangelo captures him 'dramaturgically' at the moment when he becomes a 'statue', the moment when David first glimpses Goliath and considers how to vanquish him: Where must I hurl the stone? At such a moment a person is poised in the utter repose of reflection and contemplation, turning, dramaturgically speaking, into a statue. A similar thing can be said of Michelangelo's *Moses*. He is shown at the moment when he grasps what he has already learnt from Yahweh, that the people are dancing round the Golden Calf. Still amazed, his wrath just beginning to stir, he stands there, holding the Tablets of the Law in his hand, but the next moment he will leap to his feet and shatter them and order the death of three thousand men of his people—that is dramaturgical thinking in sculpture. And so, dramaturgically speaking, my *Crucifixions* posed the question: How do I depict a crucifixion *today*? The cross has become a symbol and thus usable even as adornment, for example, as a crucifix between a woman's breasts. The notion that the cross was once an instrument of martyrdom has been lost. In my first *Crucifixion* I attempt with the dance round the cross to make it into a cross again, into the scandalous object it once represented. In the second *Crucifixion* the cross has been replaced by a still crueller instrument of martyrdom, the wheel, and not one but many people have been broken upon it; only one person is crucified—a decapitated pregnant woman with a child dangling from her slit-open body. Rats scramble about on the grisly scaffolds. In the third *Crucifixion* rats swarm over a fat crucified Jew with severed arms. It is not an infatuation with horror that gave rise to these images. Countless people have died in incomparably more horrible ways than Jesus of Nazareth. The scandal for us should not be the crucified god but the crucified person. Death, however awful, can never be as horrible for a god as for a person—the god will be resurrected. Thus the scandal of Christianity today is no longer the cross but the resurrection, and this is the only way to understand the work *Resurrection* from 1978. Not a radiant god is resurrected but a mummy, with no witnesses. There is a parallel here with my dramatic work: in *The Meteor* (1966) the scandal consists in the fact that a person repeatedly dies and is repeatedly resurrected. Precisely because he experiences the miracle in the flesh, he is unable to believe in it. The *Angels* were a different matter. In 1952, a penniless writer, I borrowed my way to a house in Neuchâtel. It was quite difficult. Who wanted, even then, to lend money to a writer? The life-insurance company Pax, which gave me the first mortgage, terminated it immediately. But we managed to move into the house, helped by those who could. That was when I produced my two gouaches, *The Astronomers* and *Drowned Couple*, a technique which I did not use again until 1978 (*The World of Atlases*). I painted at night, and at two in the morning a bat always visited me, a delightful creature I dubbed Mathilde. One day I acted unfairly—I shut the window and went about catching Mathilde. Once I had caught her, I showed her to the children and explained to them that Mathilde was a mouse angel. Then I let her go. She was extremely offended and never showed her face again. After that the angel motif obsessed me. It was less mockery than high jinks. Mathilde's revenge—I drew countless human angels and even egg-laying cherubim off the cuff, as caricatures. My sense of humour seduced me. This factor—the one central to me—should never be underestimated; it operates everywhere. Only gradually did I realize that angels are in fact fearsome beings which Mathilde resembles as a lizard does Tyrannosaurus Rex. I began to take a dramaturgical interest in how an angel could be depicted today, for even in art few angels convince me, except perhaps the swooping, striking, savage angels of Albrecht Dürer's *Apocalypse*. And so I tried to depict angels dramaturgically, the two *Angels of Death* and the *Angel*, on which I worked for a long time— angels too are things of terror. Though Elisabeth Brock-Sulzer wrote of 'Dürrenmatt's early mezzotint technique' in connection with my ink drawings and insisted on seeing my later drawings—for example, the quick ballpoint sketches from nature—as a 'liberation', I can't agree with her. Those drawings are conventional, not dramaturgical. Any painter could do better. They were a caprice, finger exercises if you will, just as I once spent weeks making collages or repeatedly turned to caricature. The technique I developed in my ink drawings represents my graphic 'continuity'—this is where my experience lies, where development can be seen. Personally I prefer painting. But painting tears me away from my work while my ink drawings take form at my desk, the ballpoint sketches too, of course. In this way the *Minotaur* series was quickly completed—I often worked on it early in the morning, after agonizing over my writing all night. And my first *Self-Portrait* was painted at five in the morning—I depicted myself staring into the shaving mirror. By contrast, I spend an average of fourteen days working on an ink drawing. Many I take up again later and rework them. The *Pope* scenes are also meant dramaturgically, not blasphemously—after all, it's a scandalous thing for someone to claim to be Christ's deputy on earth, infallible, etc. I recall a discussion of *The Deputy* (1963)[1] on television in which Rolf Hochhuth was accosted by a priest: Wasn't he ashamed of the fact that *The Deputy* offended millions of believers for whom the pope is sacred? The priest should have been asked whether he was ashamed of the fact that the pope's pretensions offend those who don't believe them. I don't believe them. Christianity that does not conceive of itself as a scandal has no more justification. The pope is the symbol of theology and thus of dogmatism, the belief that one is in possession of the truth. People who hold this belief are quarrelsome. That is why there are always many popes—religious and political—and that is why the quarrels among them never end. Again and again truth stands against truth, until the last pope rides off on the mammoth of his might, vanishing into the ice-age night of humanity (*The Last Pope*). As for the *Tower of Babel* drawings, my dramaturgical concern was to convey the height of the tower. The Tower of Babel has been depicted many times—for example

[1] Play by German dramatist Rolf Hochhuth (1931–), which caused a scandal by criticizing Pope Pius XII's role in the Second World War.

in Bruegel's paintings. But the tower was always too small for me. It was never *the* tower. In my drawings one clearly sees the curvature of the earth, in relation to which the tower in the first drawing is nearly six thousand miles high. The 'cloud' reaching down is cosmic dust that licks the earth. In the background is the sun as it appears when we block out the red hydrogen end of the spectrum. Since my small-town childhood I have been interested in astronomy; later physics entered into my thinking; and today I amuse myself mainly with one of its sub-disciplines, cosmology, where modernity carries on the pre-Socratic tradition. Thus all my *Tower of Babel* pictures show the senselessness of building a tower that reaches the sky, and thus the absurdity of all human endeavour. The Tower of Babel is the emblem of human hubris. It collapses, and with it the human world. What humanity will leave behind is its debris. The *Tower of Babel* drawings IV and V show this collapse. At the same time, the end of the inhabited world has come. The star that explodes in *Tower of Babel IV* is a supernova. What remains is a white point, a neutron star, a star of infinite density. Galaxies in various stages of genesis and decay become visible and vast black holes palpable. They signify the final states of stars, which in turn could (perhaps) be the beginning of new worlds. The motif of the world's end is bound up with the death motif—each person who dies experiences the end of his world. It is not surprising that the executioner plays a role in my drawings, as in my plays; it would be surprising if he were missing. In our day and age the human being has assumed the role of the good old Grim Reaper. The human executioner is Godfather Death no longer. But sometimes I find Arthur Schopenhauer's idea illuminating, that the individual's life is like a sea wave—it passes, but new waves arise. I cannot think that I will one day be 'no more'. I can imagine that I will 'always' be someone. Always someone different. Always a new consciousness, so that one day I too will experience the end of the world. And thus the end of the world is of perpetual timeliness. I rendered this motif for the stage in *Portrait of a Planet* (1970). I conceived the text as an acting exercise, trying to express as much as possible with minimal dramaturgical means. Before writing, I depicted the motif using mixed media (*Portrait of a Planet II*). During the Vietnam War, the photograph of a man holding a head in each hand was published in many different magazines. At the bottom left is a gutted space capsule in which two American astronauts lost their lives. *The World Butcher* is a figure from the first version of the play. And so my dramaturgical approach to writing, drawing and painting is an attempt to find increasingly final figures, final artistic forms. For example, I arrived at the Atlas motif by way of the Sisyphus motif. The first *Sisyphus* gouache came about in 1946, at the same time as *Pilate*. I left the university and announced that I was going to become a painter. It would have been rash to give writing as my goal. I painted the two pictures as a sort of alibi, to prove to my fellow students that I was serious about painting. Simultaneously I wrote the stories 'Pilate' and 'The Image of Sisyphus'. All I'd like to note on *Sisyphus* is that I was mainly concerned with what compels Sisyphus to keep pushing the rock up the hill. Maybe it is the revenge he takes on the gods—he exposes their injustice. With *Pilate*, meanwhile, I was obsessed by the idea that Pilate knew from the beginning that a god was standing before him, and was convinced from the beginning that this god had come to kill him. By contrast, Atlas is a mythological figure who today, paradoxically enough, can be depicted again at last—a man carrying the firmament seems to contradict our world view. But if we picture the world's initial state as a vast compact sphere the size of Neptune's orbit (March), or as a black hole leading to the Big Bang, or if the final state of a world in its implosion from excess weight looms before us as the vision of an immensely heavy sphere, this view of the world makes Atlas again a mythological possibility but at the same time the ultimate image of the man carrying—forced to carry—the world, his world. It is no coincidence that my latest play *The Appointed Time* (1977) came about at the same time as several Atlas pictures, as it deals with two people in Atlas' situation: the first tries to carry the world; the second doesn't want to carry it but in the end must carry it onward. Admittedly, the first Atlas image goes back to 1958, *Atlas Failing*. The most important thing in this image of the world's end is the people. They carry signs: Atlas needn't fail, Atlas mustn't fail, Atlas can't fail . . . the one who wrote 'Atlas will fail' has been beheaded. The foreseeable catastrophe comes to pass or, in stronger terms, foreseeable catastrophes come to pass. The drawing with the peculiar title *The Glass Coffins of the Dead Shall Be the Battering Rams* expresses the idea that everything comes back to roost. Put in dramaturgical terms—things take the worst possible turn. My recurring depiction of the worst possible turn has nothing to do with pessimism and nothing to do with monomania. The worst possible turn is that which can be depicted dramaturgically, it is, on the stage, exactly what in sculpture makes *David* a statue and my pictures dramaturgical pictures. *The Catastrophe*, for example. This picture shows more than a train crash and the ensuing chain reaction—up above, the sun simultaneously collides with another heavenly body. Six minutes later the earth will cease to exist. Here too—the worst possible turn, the attempt to depict not a catastrophe but *the* catastrophe. What is depictable is not the thing in itself but images in themselves. The last rendition of the Atlas motif, *The World of Atlases*, is one of my favourite pictures. It came about on a whim. Side by side on my studio wall I stuck two hundred-by-seventy-one-centimetre sheets, my favourite format for gouaches. I meant to do a quick sketch. That was in 1965. I've been working on the picture ever since. I should have known. I've never done a sketch for any of my pictures. Here it is reproduced as it was on 10 June 1978. It shows Atlases playing with globes. The heavier a world is, the smaller it is in its final state. The Atlases in the foreground gasp for breath beneath their globes. I should note that the impression of a night landing at the New York airport played a role as well, when I first realized how hellish it must be to live in an overpopulated world. As for my portraits, they were completed quickly, except the first two. I'm glad that I succeeded in producing at least a painted portrait of Walter Mehring[2]—I still haven't managed a written one. In much of his late poetry, this powerful writer has outlived not himself but us. Otto Riggenbach (*Portrait of a Psychiatrist*) is captured in conversation with my wife. He is one of the few friends we have in Neuchâtel and owns some of Auberjonois's[3] best paintings. The most spontaneous effort was the *Portrait of My Wife*, taking just ten minutes, in Ste-Maxime on the Côte d'Azur. It was an especially happy time for us. There we thought we had acquired the house we were looking for, though fortunately the purchase fell through in the end after all. In her elation my wife didn't notice that I was sketching her. In Ste-Maxime, somewhat earlier, in 1958, I also produced the ink drawing with a self-portrait, *St Tropez*—the thought that people were being tortured and murdered on the other side of the Mediterranean oppressed me. Unfortunately the drawing has lost none of its relevance. I painted the actor Leonard Steckel

2 Walter Mehring (1896–1981): Socially critical writer, best known for his Weimar-era satires.

3 René Auberjonois (1872–1957): Swiss post-impressionist painter.

from memory in 1965. The portrait of Varlin was drawn on 22 October 1977. It was the last day I spent with him. We talked about painting. He told me he regarded Matisse as the greatest painter of our time. He said, 'The sad thing about painting: you stand in front of a canvas, pick up a brush, and already the canvas is spoiled.' Then he drew me, several times, crossing everything out again. He let one drawing stand and gave it to me. Then he said he would go to sleep and I should draw him. When he woke up he asked to see the drawing. He asked me if that was really how he looked. I gave no reply, and Varlin said it wouldn't be much longer then. He died on 30 October. *Portrait of a Hotelier* shows my friend Hans Liechti, hotelkeeper and art collector in Zäziwill, a forty-five-minute walk from the village where I was born. Like me, he ended up in Neuenburg. After writing I often sit with him long into the night, telling him what I'm writing, and drawing what one can draw. I don't know if I'd still draw and paint without him. His enthusiasm for painting has a productive effect. His portrait was done on a Sunday afternoon. He'd been cooking, at lunch his restaurant had been packed, then relatives had come, and that evening he had a banquet in the upstairs dining room. He came to my studio in his work clothes to have a rest. He left me not an hour later to go stand at his stove again and I finished painting the picture. At ten in the evening I called him to come. He came, still in his work clothes, and was pleased with me. My most recent ink drawings are portraits as well: *Wrathful God*—who can fail to understand his wrath? (I completed the ink drawing at Liechti's with a kitchen knife.) Mazdak was the founder of a communist sect. Around 530 CE, the Persian emperor rammed three thousand of his followers into the ground head first—thus planting their ideas in the soil. Though a person can be killed, the idea lives on. Leprous, mad Ophelia's child will be neither leprous nor mad. Vultures castrate the Cossack Mazeppa, bound atop a horse. He lives on in poems. *Chronos Castrating Uranus*— only thus could time begin its reign; the mythological depiction of the Big Bang. In *Labyrinths* I picked up on a motif that also fascinates me as a writer. I first addressed it in the novella *The City* (1952), and am addressing it now in the story 'The Winter War in Tibet'. The labyrinth comes with the *Minotaur*. He is a monster, and as such he is the image of the isolated individual. The individual faces a murky, impenetrable world—the labyrinth is the world seen by the Minotaur. And so the *Minotaur* works show the Minotaur without the experience of the Other, the You. All he knows is how to rape and kill. He doesn't perish at Theseus' hand, he crawls off to die like an animal. Theseus is unable to track him down. The Minotaur's murder is a legend. The figure of the Minotaur gave rise, by association, to the *World Bull*, using a somewhat different technique because the paper permitted no other. The *World Bull* is the symbol of the rampaging monster we call world history. The work *The Two Animals* presents a paraphrase of Manichaeism, resurgent these days, the belief that world history is a struggle between two principles, good and evil. The two dinosaurs which have sunk their teeth into each other in the background are both equally obstinate. Of course there are non-dramaturgical works as well, associations relating to literary motifs such as *Escape I* and *Escape II*, which first took shape in *The Tunnel* and *The Trap*. *The Battle of the Two Old Men* shows how hatred goes on raging even when it has lost its motivation. I never learnt how to draw or paint. I still don't know how to do oil paintings. The only person I asked 'How do you paint in oils, anyway?' was Anna Keel.[3] And she told me: 'Use petrol.' I did all the oil paintings in 1966. The fact

3 Anna Keel (1940–2010): Swiss painter and sculptor

that my *Bank* paintings are also done in oil and petrol is not meant as a critique of the Swiss banking system. On the contrary, the dignified end I provide (*Last General Meeting of the Swiss Bank*) was meant to improve my credit standing with our banks, at least I hope so, as I need it more than ever now that—as I recently read in the *Brückenbauer*[4]—I no longer exist for the critics, literarily speaking. Since then I have returned to watercolours, however. My *Bank* pictures make it especially clear that my drawings and paintings are not rooted solely in dramaturgical considerations. They are the echo of my comedy *Frank the Fifth* (1967), the opera of a private bank, a play that was never successfully staged— there is a new version lying in my desk drawer. *The Tower of Babel* and the works *Narses in Captivity* and *Byzantine Saints* with its Byzantine motifs also go back to a fragment or to a work that was subsequently destroyed—drawing as a compensatory act. But of course there are other connections between my literary and graphic work. Every act of depiction, in whatever media, presupposes a backdrop of impressions, images and thought. Today this backdrop is no longer universal, unless one presents oneself as a leftist, a Catholic, both simultaneously, etc. In general contemporary writers as well as contemporary painters are unconsciously seeking an ideology, something universal. I have always refused to let myself be reduced to a common denominator. Inevitably this means there are few who understand me. On their own no one would guess the premises of my literary work or of my pictures, for they lie in my way of thinking, which is essentially epistemological, and in my sense of humour, which is per se subjective. Thus people prefer not to take me seriously; otherwise they would have to make the mental effort to follow. I am a conscious loner. I don't belong to

4 *Wir Brückenbauer*: Swiss weekly magazine.

the avant-garde. Anyone who belongs to it these days is
trotting along in a herd. And so the associations from which
my pictures are constructed are the results of my personal
mental adventures, not of a universal mental method. I
don't paint surrealistic pictures—surrealism is an ideology—
I paint pictures which are intelligible to me. I paint for
myself. That is why I am not a painter. I confront our time,
and our time can't be tackled with words alone. Thinking
in concepts, the methods of mathematics, the necessary
abstraction of scientific thinking cannot be depicted
abstractly in visual art. There is nothing more abstract than
a formula. It is the ultimate possible abstraction. $E = mc^2$,
for example. Mathematics has a capacity for abstraction that
ceases to be concrete, that inevitably breaks out of concrete-
ness. It is impossible to represent the theory of relativity in
a non-abstract manner unless one does so in sensory allegories. But sensory allegories are not geometric or stereometric forms, they are myths—our myths, Atlas enabled.
My first drawings may have been influenced by Bosch, the
grotesque images of the beginning (*The Horsemen of the
Apocalypse*, *The World as Theatre*), even before I became a
writer. But I do not seek the symbolism Bosch found. What
I seek—in my writing and my drawing—are the images and
allegories that are still possible in the age of science, an age
that succeeded where philosophy failed: to describe reality
abstractly. If we need four or *n* dimensions, we need them
because the facts of reality can't be described in any other
way. We have no way of simplifying these highly complex
relationships and facts. Nuclear physics can't be represented
in popular language. It can only be paraphrased in popular
language. It must be thought through to be grasped. There
is no retreat into simplicity. Something which by nature is
not concrete can be represented only through allegories.
Thus abstract art—when it works—is poetic at best, the

beauty of lines. It is pure form and thus pure aesthetics. Never was painting more aesthetic than today. What it passes off as its meaning is merely asserted, not integrated. To represent this art as an 'intellectual statement' is nonsense. Again and again—I am not a painter. In terms of technique I paint like a child, but I don't think like a child. I paint for the same reason I write—because I think. Painting as the art of making 'beautiful pictures' doesn't interest me, any more than the art of making 'beautiful theatre' interests me. I could never be a full-time painter for the simple reason that most of the time I wouldn't know what to paint. I am a graphic dilettante. As a student I lived in Bern in a room I'd painted. Above the bed was a grotesque crucifixion, alongside it scenes from my first, never-published play from which another drawing exists, one of my earliest. And so my painting and drawing is a complement to my writing—for all the things I can only express visually. For this reason there is little work of mine that is purely 'illustrative'. When writing, too, I proceed not from a problem but from images. The origin is always the image, the situation—the world. Incidentally, I am still astounded at Daniel Keel's[5] mad notion to publish this book and still abashed at the fact that Manuel Gasser,[6] to whom painting owes so much, actually wrote the foreword for it, and—I must admit—I am actually rather proud that he has not pronounced awful judgement upon my paintings and drawings.

5 Daniel Keel (1930–2011): Founder of the Swiss publishing house Diogenes, regarded as Dürrenmatt's discoverer.

6 Manuel Gasser (1909–79): Swiss journalist and art critic.

FINGER EXERCISES ON THE PRESENT

1952

Ladies and Gentlemen,

If one is going to commit the quixotry, in so small a country as ours, of being a German-language writer and nothing but, not three-quarters or four-fifths still an editor, teacher or farmer or whatever other professions we have here, one might want to ask whether such an endeavour, which by nature revolves round bankruptcy more or less like the earth round the sun, is absolutely and under all circumstances necessary. After all, not even all our country's people speak German, and to those who do the language is generally somewhat alien, as they speak dialect, naturally enough, and the country where seventy million Germans live has gone under and broken apart. Wanting to be a writer in this day and age means running your head against the wall. Ladies and gentlemen, I do this with a passion; it is my view that walls were invented for this very purpose. I have become a writer in this country *precisely because* writing is not needed here. I did so to become a nuisance to people. Am I a good writer? I don't know, and I'm not much concerned with this pointless question, but I hope it will be said of me that I was an uncomfortable writer. And so the idea of addressing mainly the Germans doesn't even cross my mind; it is above all the Swiss I address, above all—as you happen to be sitting in front of me—it is you, ladies and gentlemen. Some will object that Switzerland is a province and those who address a province are provincial writers. Even assuming such a thing still as provinces, those who say this are wrong. One can view the world today only from the back of beyond.

THEOREMS ON THE THEATRE

1970

1. *Theatre and Reality.* How does theatre stand in relation to reality? Reality is everything that occurs. Theatre occurs as well. Both are events. But the event that is theatre occurs infinitely less often than the sum of all other events which with it makes up the whole of reality. Reality would get by without theatre, it would get by without people; and in principle people would get by without theatre. That they do occasionally practise it or concern themselves with it must therefore have something to do with the structure of human reality. The only meaningful question is that about the relationship between the structure that is theatre and the structure of human reality.

2. This relationship is often seen as consisting in the fact that theatre depicts human reality. People imitate their reality on the stage. They become play-actors. Their act is their play. They play out reality instead of letting it occur.

3. If this relationship between theatre and reality holds true, theatre must be defined even in its rudiments, and not only in its sophisticated forms, as an imitation of reality—more than just historically reconstructable (and thus hypothetical), its origins must be demonstrable in the present as well.

4. Children imitate their reality in their play. They play teacher, they assume different roles. But this play is not yet theatre. An integral part of theatre is the players' consciousness of playing

not for themselves but for an audience. This kind of theatre often arises spontaneously too, a process which we especially observe in sports. In itself sport is not theatre, although spectators are present. Two boxers fight one another; the fight is a real fight, even if certain rules must be observed. So-called freestyle wrestling is a different matter. For the freestyle wrestler anything goes. The fight is supposed to be still more brutal than boxing and thus veers into theatre. A freestyle wrestler must step forward each evening like an actor; because the audience demands of him the fiercest and most ruthless possible fight, this fight must be imitated. Hence the fight seems more brutal than it is. The extent to which freestyle wrestling is already theatre can also be seen in the different roles the wrestlers play. The evil and the cowardly, the invincible and the sadistic. They perform under various names: OK Stateless, Golden Apollo, the Vienna Strangler; a fellow from Lesser Basel called himself Count Adolf von Krupp in the US and had a butler in tails spray the ring with perfume before he deigned to enter it.

5. Freestyle wrestling illustrates one of the most important rules for actors. The freestyle wrestler must play not just the cause but also the effect. Not only must he seem to mete out blows, he must also seem to take them. The greater the impact of a blow, the greater its artistic impact. In acting terms—an actor must know not just how to speak but also how to listen, not just how to murder but also how to be murdered.

6. If we define theatre as the conscious imitation of a human reality, we must ask which specific human realities theatre is able to imitate directly. In his day, Aristotle correctly described theatre as the imitation of a human action (action understood as a sequence of events that is 'extended' in time).

7. For this reason only a human action of the same duration as the imitated action can be imitated directly. Strictly speaking, the infamous unity of time, place and action applies only when a human event is directly imitable. This is true of very few actions in which people become involved or which they trigger. People live in time, and their actions span 'temporal distances' exceeding those of a theatrical evening.

8. In the clown we observe a primal theatre similar to that of freestyle wrestling. The clown also performs an action on the stage, the struggle between people and objects and their astoundingly ingenuous failure to cope with the simplest things—Grock[1] pushes the grand piano closer to the bench so that he can play more easily.

9. If freestyle wrestling, by imitating a fight which has a winner and a loser, embodies the primal form of tragedy, the clown embodies the primal form of comedy. Both primal forms can be expanded to include any number of players. There is such a thing as four-person freestyle wrestling, while the simple actions which Karl Valentin and Liesl Karlstadt[2] featured on their stage are genuine artworks of language and acting.

10. The more complex and temporally extended an action one attempts to imitate onstage, the more dramaturgical contrivances are required. This explains why today's dramatic avant-garde seems to be regressing as far as technique is concerned. Primal theatre arises instinctively; modern theatre consciously returns to primal theatre—indeed it tries to be even less than primal theatre, nothing but theatre as such. Peter Handke, in his *Offending the Audience* (1966), has

[1] Grock (1880–1959): Born Charles Adrien Wettach, the most renowned European clown of his day.

[2] Karl Valentin (1882–1948) and Liesl Karlstadt (1892–1960): Germany's greatest twentieth-century comic duo.

gone the farthest here. For better understanding, this significant work is best compared with so-called concrete painting. As I understand it, this art movement seeks to hew to the 'two-dimensionality' of the canvas. It abandons the attempt to depict a three-dimensional reality on this canvas. Hence the only concrete things can be lines, surfaces, colours and the interplay among them. No longer tied to content, it is nothing now but form. By abandoning perspective and with it the artistic contrivance of simulating space by painterly means, it falls into a world of pure forms which permits only variations on these forms. The freedom of concrete art lies in its endless scope for variation.

11. This is also true of Handke's *Offending the Audience*. By having the actors cease imitating and instead merely move and speak, and by varying this movement and speech arbitrarily, he achieves a concrete theatre that no longer imitates anything, except in the final scene in which he has the actors berate the audience. This conclusion, which gives the play its name, is no longer concrete; it is meant as a provocation and, strictly speaking, is no longer a part of the play, any more than the pedestal on which an abstract sculpture stands is a part of the sculpture.

12. The same applies to Handke's famous 'Reizwörter' (Loaded Words, 1970). They enrage that segment of the audience that lets itself be enraged. This audience is angered not by the loaded word itself but, rightfully, by the fact that it hears the loaded word from an actor on the stage. By speaking the loaded words onstage, the actors imitate provocateurs who intend to anger the audience, in which they fortunately succeed with an audience that naively goes along with them—this audience is still the most rewarding—while an audience that is not enraged by the loaded words is also right not to be enraged because it is not so naive as to believe that the actors trying to enrage it are really provocateurs. To become enraged, this audience would have to imitate the audience that becomes enraged; that is, the spectators who aren't enraged must, in order to become enraged, play the role that Handke assigns them—they would have to play the philistines who, since they don't become enraged, they are not; it is a role which doesn't suit them, since they don't want to be philistines, which is why they applaud. At Handke's plays everyone who isn't a philistine or doesn't want to be a philistine applauds. Once word has gotten out, everyone applauds.

13. If it is true that in the non-provocative part of his play Handke is no longer imitating anything, the question is not only whether this aspect is still theatre but also whether theatre that no longer imitates anything can still be theatre at all. Actors in such a piece could no longer be compared to actors but to circus performers, tightrope walkers, trapeze artists and jugglers. Just as they negotiate tightropes, swing on trapezes and juggle balls, the actors negotiate difficult passages, swing on syllogisms and juggle loaded words. Yet this comparison does not entirely hold water. Even if the actors of *Offending the Audience* are not imitating an action, they are imitating Handke and reciting his lines. Handke of all playwrights requires great directors. He composes wonderfully difficult scores. Ultimately *Offending the Audience* proves to be a brilliant dead end, since as a dramatic form it permits of endless variation. And in *Kaspar* (1967) Handke already beats a retreat. *Kaspar* already imitates an action—the power which language exerts over people. *Kaspar* is already a didactic play. It seeks to show something. It demonstrates something. But even as a demonstration *Kaspar* is unique. The play demonstrates something that can be demonstrated only in the theatre. Like his *Offending the Audience* or Samuel Beckett's *Waiting for Godot* (1953), Handke's

Kaspar is a dramaturgical egg of Columbus laid by the hen of drama on the modern stage. Beckett and Handke are lucky flukes at risk of falling victim to themselves. Woe to their imitators!

14. *Beckett.* When we search for the dramaturgical aspects that govern his works, it becomes clear that the terms 'reality' and 'imitation' get us nowhere. Samuel Beckett has a great deal in common with Karl Valentin. He does popular theatre for intellectuals and people who take themselves for such. It is astonishing how little thought he demands from the audience, compared, for example, with Lessing;[3] he is far more immediate and thus more culinary. The dramatic contrivances he uses are relatively simple, a pause perhaps to bridge a span of time—that is all. What counts is the situation and the dialogues—but what a situation and what dialogues! Yet is it still reality Beckett imitates? Isn't it rather that he uses drama to present symbols that can be seen as an allegory of reality? Shouldn't we drop the terms 'imitation' and 'reality' in order to give dramaturgy (not drama, which does so on its own) the chance to grasp the theatre? In our dramaturgy we are thrown back to the starting point. We will be forced to do so many times to come—dramaturgy consists of reversals.

15. *Drama and Possibility.* In Christian Dietrich Grabbe's[4] *Napoleon, or the Hundred Days* (1831), Act 5, Scene 2, there is an incident which, while probably not unusual at the time, is unusual for the way in which Grabbe depicts it. Two Berliners are arguing near Wavre:

---

3 Gotthold Ephraim Lessing (1729–81): Writer, philosopher and dramatist of the German Enlightenment.

4 Christian Dietrich Grabbe (1801–36): German playwright, pioneer of realism.

EFRAIM. You dog, even if a Jew I am, I am a citizen and a Berlin volunteer like you—there!

He gives the Berliner a resounding slap. The Berliner is about to return it when a cannonball rips off Efraim's head.

BERLINER (*dives to the side*). Oh, how cruelly Fate treats me!

16. This scene makes us laugh. *Napoleon* is a historical play. It is based on a historical event and thus on a historical reality. But it's hard for us to regard the scene quoted above as a 'real event'. The scene is so good that we suspect Grabbe of having invented it. Historical drama may be based on happenings that were once reality but evidently not in all its parts. This observation also forces us to rethink the relationship between drama and reality.

17. In his writings on poetics, of which unfortunately we have only a fragment—unfortunately, because it contains the first dramaturgical theory we know of—Aristotle writes that the poet's task is to relate not what has happened but what could happen. Unlike the historian, the dramatist relates not what Alcibiades did but what he could have done. Here Aristotle expresses the relationship between drama and reality more precisely than we have done so far. It is not reality as such that is 'imitated' but rather the possibility, and in principle it does not matter whether this possibility was reality. According to Aristotle, the relationship between drama and reality is the same as the relationship between possibility and reality.

18. With this Aristotle not only expands drama's object, he adds to this object a subjective element. People regard as possible only what they believe could occur; the possibility people believe in depends on their interpretation of reality. For the ancient Greeks, a plague could be a god's punishment inflicted upon Thebes because the city's king killed his father and married his mother. For us, the plague is a medical development whose causes are to be sought in poor hygiene. While the Greeks see the plague's end as a god's response to Oedipus' atonement, which makes this development possible, we see it as a mere aesthetic phenomenon—*deus ex machina*—a phenomenon which we accept out of respect for Sophocles and which we are educated enough not to be bothered by. We do not associate the outbreak and disappearance of the plague with the wrath and appeasement of a god. Thus Aristotle rightly equates the plot of tragedy with myth, while leaving it open whether this holds true for him, the thinker, or only for the audience. It definitely holds true for the audience. Each audience reacts differently to the plays it is confronted with; in a time such as ours which thinks historically, in the theatre too, and stages the plays of all times, this fact is often overlooked, and often makes us overlook the audacities of the classics because they have become classics for us, and because literature harbours an aesthetic cult of personality comparable only to the political personality cults of the Soviet Union and China. Our Goethe who art in Heaven. The credo we parrot is that the great dramas of literature are timeless and thus perfect and sacred. We forget that possibility as the object of drama means something other for a Greek than for Calderón,[5] for Calderón something other than for Shakespeare, for Shakespeare something other than for Brecht, etc.

19. Accordingly, the message of a play is variable. This poses a difficulty especially for actors and directors. They don't believe in a play, like the literati and the audience—they interpret it. They transport it onto the stage they find before them. What once was reasonable can turn paradoxical.

5 Pedro Calderón de la Barca (1600–81): Spanish Baroque playwright.

What once posed a political problem is one no longer and is thus no longer recognized as a political problem. A famous example is the scene from *King Lear*. Goethe's contemporaries found this scene so preposterous that they cut it. Today, it is often seen as a harbinger of the Theatre of the Absurd that serves only to set the plot in motion. In reality, this opening scene of one of the greatest tragedies we know is political. Lear is a great king, a hero who has failed at one thing alone—fathering a son. Lear divides his kingdom among his daughters so that in his old age he can enjoy his power rather than have to assert it. His political error lies in the belief that he has established an orderly world. But what it meant to have no son in the age of feudalism is shown by the many wars of succession fought for that very reason. Lear is a king who wants to retire in a world which he believes is orderly but which is in fact disorderly. Lear is like an Atlas who wants to rest—as he drops the world, it buries him. Of course this initial political situation is merely the premise of the play and, just as the opening moves of a chess match do not make up its greatness, the opening of a play says little about its significance. Still, it is important to see them as a precondition for the further course of the plot.

20. But, as far as drama is concerned, we have called into question not only the term 'reality', which Aristotle does not use, but the term 'imitation' with which Aristotle operates. For Aristotle, tragedy is the imitation of a possible action. But though he expands the object of the imitation, as we have described, he restricts it again with the term 'imitation'; more precisely, his interpreters have restricted it.

21. It is easy to see why Aristotle worked with the concept of imitation. As the first dramaturgical theorist, he took as the object of his investigation the art he found before him—Attic tragedy. He postulated a theory about this construct. To understand Aristotle as a dramaturgical theorist one must thus examine the theatrical preconditions of Attic tragedy, even if this calls into question his theory's general applicability. After all, an actor on buskins and wearing a mask with a speaking tube is quite a different matter from a present-day actor without a mask. Depending on their masks, actors were either tragic or comic, lacking the ability to switch from tragic to comic as actors without masks can; they were fixed, their movements severely stylized, probably also set by tradition as in Noh theatre. Onstage they could neither eat nor murder without looking ridiculous (Euripides was the first to hint at such naturalistic effects); they could only set actions in motion. Each action had to take place behind the scenes if only because the action could not be represented directly—it had to be transformed into a static episode. Possibilities included speech and response; messengers' reports and laments over past events; prophecies and commands. With good reason, the attempt to restore Attic tragedy with its chants led to opera and not to plays. For Aristotle (as for the Greeks in general), poetry was thus imitation; in tragedy, actors wearing masks could not imitate characters but only stylized people, mythological figures. It was left to comedy to depict ordinary or even 'base' characters (which of course soon became types), on which Aristotle commented, with a glance at painting: 'It follows that we must represent men either as better than in real life, or as worse, or as they are. It is the same in painting. Polygnotus depicted men as nobler than they are, Pauson as less noble, Dionysius drew them true to life.'[6]

22. But even a term that is incorrect in a particular case, and in general, can bring insight. Actors with masks were agents whose characters were determined by the myth.

---

6 Aristotle, *Poetics* (Samuel Henry Butcher trans.) (New York: Dover Books, 1997), p. 11.

Thus Aristotle's distinction among the different characters also refers to the fixed character of the mythical figures. This is why the action becomes so important for him, paradoxically, given that the action was exactly what the Attic stage could represent only indirectly. Aristotle writes:

> For Tragedy is an imitation, not of men but of an action and of life, and life consists in action, and its end is a mode of action, not a quality. Now character determines men's qualities, but it is by their actions that they are happy or the reverse. Dramatic action, therefore, is not with a view to the representation of character: character comes in as subsidiary to the actions. Hence the incidents and the plot are the end of a tragedy; and the end is the chief thing of all. Again, without action there cannot be a tragedy; there may be without character.[7]

According to this, plot for Aristotle is enabled by myth, dependent on myth. The myth is the given, the familiar. A familiar myth is more effective than an invented plot because it doesn't seem arbitrary, and without its mythic background a form as artificial and extreme as that of Attic tragedy becomes hollow declamation. That is exactly why, as a form, it is a product of its time. Over time, as Greek mythology ceased to be the stuff of tradition and became the stuff of education, new plots had to be invented if drama was to retain its immediacy.

23. It is well known that the French classical dramatists were the most stubborn in maintaining Aristotle's unity. They saw the unity of place, time and action not as a dramaturgical possibility that could be realized only under certain circumstances but as the very ideal of plot. They attempted to live up to this ideal or at least approximate it

7 Ibid., p. 27.

as closely as possible. For example, the action had to happen within the space of one day. Though the place did not always have to be the same room, the different rooms in which the action would unfold over the space of one day had to be located in the same palace, etc. The reason is easily apparent. Everything courtly tends towards stylization; rules become laws. Attic tragedy was theatre for the people, the myths 'imitated' were familiar ones; the theatre of Corneille and Racine[8] was court theatre. Court rituals replaced popular myths, rhetoric pathos, the artificial, the elementary; with them, Aristotle's unity has the effect of an old-fashioned pigtail which Lessing, in his *Hamburg Dramaturgy* (1767–79), is right to chop off. If Aristotle's unity were a universal law, Attic comedy would have to obey it as well. Yet the comedies of Cratinus[9] and Aristophanes lived from creativity, not from myth. They proceeded from political situations and events which they elevated to a universal level. They no longer imitated myths; they produced myths. The first step from imitative to representational theatre had been taken.

24. There is only one law to be discerned in Attic tragedy—the unity of stage, material and form. These three factors (which comprise further factors) depend on, determine, justify one another. On stage a given material is represented by playing it. Performance and play are never identical. A performance is a play more or less fully realized on stage; a play is a more or less precise blueprint for a performance. But the three factors of stage, material and form must affect even the writing of a play, as the flexible framework within which dramaturgical thought and instinct operate. To write is always to conceptualize a performance, be it a future,

8 Pierre Corneille (1606–84) and Jean Racine (1639–99): Pre-eminent seventeenth-century French tragedians.

9 Cratinus (519–422 BCE): Master of Athenian Old Comedy, contemporary of Aristophanes.

utopian one; without this conceptualization, the dramatic form is meaningless. Stage, material and form influence one another. (Theatre is always a unity, a result; these three factors represent nothing but a working hypothesis, and not an especially exact one, a system into which additional factors can be incorporated by filing them under one of the three factors, whereby the stage seems to cover the stage itself and any necessary changes in location, while the material covers the plot, and the form comprises acting style, language, structure, the passing of time, etc.) Take Shakespeare. The Globe Theatre had a primitive stage, 'a scaffolding where one saw little, where everything merely signified'.[10] The facade of the stage house with its doors and galleries served as a backdrop; the open-air stage was surrounded on three sides by the audience. In essence, its construction resembled the stage of Attic tragedy but it was employed differently with regard to material and form (we will pass over the very different historical background, though without denying its primary significance). Shakespeare's materials span longer periods of time and require various different settings such as interiors, streets, battlefields, etc. The place had to be broken down into different locations, the time into different intervals and the action into episodes. Accordingly, the stage is divided into different arenas: interiors could be played inside the doors of the stage house, balcony scenes or observation posts on the gallery, crowd scenes on the stage. Thus, despite the similar stage, the 'three factors' differ from those of Attic tragedy as does the acting (as a factor subordinate to form). The rapid scene changes could be negotiated only by actors who had abandoned masks and buskins. Whereas

10 Johann Wolfgang von Goethe, 'Shakespeare als Theaterdichter' (Shakespeare as Dramatist) in *Berliner Ausgabe* (Berlin Edition), vol. 18, *Kunsttheoretische Schriften und Übersetzungen* (Writings on Art Theory and Translations) (Berlin: Aufbau Verlag, 1960), p. 147.

actors in Attic tragedy represented myths, beings larger than
life, sinister and doleful, demigods and heroes, now they
brought to the stage 'Shakespeare's great solitary figures,
bearing on their breast the star of their fate'.[11] Buskins and
masks dehumanized and abstracted the actors, made them
marionette-like, defamiliarized to the point of being primaeval, demonic, a fixed form and a voice, a mere part of the
whole; without masks the actors occupy the centre, become
human beings, represent human beings instead of merely
signifying them, and theatre too becomes human, departing
from the cultic realm. Shakespeare was an actor and wrote
for actors. On a primitive stage, using primitive devices but
superior dramaturgy, he represented people, heroes, mon-
sters and fools, poetic and realistic figures, charming and
wicked characters, harshly and without scruples, perhaps
concerned solely with mastering the material for the stage,
perhaps to criticize his violent age as well—we do not know.
The stage was left empty, the actors had at their disposal but
a few props and costumes. Playing by day, they had to
declare that it was night. They had to improvise, a pole with
a sign enough to represent a well or a forest. They murdered
because the companies were small and necessitated double
roles but they ventured the grand attempt to represent the
human world through acting alone, albeit not without
exhorting the participation of an audience that not only
desired to see its horrors and sensations but also manufac-
tured them in its imagination:

> Piece out our imperfections with your thoughts;
> Into a thousand parts divide one man,
> And make imaginary puissance;

11 Bertolt Brecht, 'A Short Organum for the Theatre' in *Brecht on Theatre: The Development of an Aesthetic* (John Willett ed. and trans.) (New
York: Hill and Wang, 1964), p. 189.

Think when we talk of horses, that you see them
Printing their proud hoofs i' the receiving earth;
For 'tis your thoughts that now must deck our kings,
Carry them here and there; jumping o'er times,
Turning the accomplishment of many years
Into an hour-glass . . .[12]

25. *Doubt.* In logic there is a law of the excluded third: A can either equal B or not equal B; there is no third possibility. The following story casts doubt on the law of the excluded third. A sultan owned a marvellous garden, and it was forbidden on pain of death to set foot there without the sultan's permission. According to a bizarre whim of the sultan, anyone who did so was allowed, before dying, to speak a truth or a lie, thus choosing the manner of his death. If he spoke a truth, he was beheaded; if he spoke a lie, he was hanged. Thus, according to the law of the excluded third, he could only be hanged or beheaded. A wise man with an interest in botany, perhaps hoping to admire a rare orchid, strolled through the garden without the sultan's permission and was arrested. Dragged in front of the sultan, he was allowed to choose the manner of death—beheading, by speaking a truth, or hanging, by speaking a lie. The wise man said, 'You will hang me,' forcing the sultan to release him, for if he had hanged him, the wise man would have said the truth and should have been beheaded; but if he had been beheaded, the wise man would have lied and should have been hanged. This way he could neither be beheaded nor hanged.

26. There are many such anecdotes questioning the idea of drama as the representation of possibility. Even the old definition of what a drama actually is points in this direction: an actor dressed as a rich lord walks across the stage; another actor, wrapped in a black cape, steps out from behind a piece

12 William Shakespeare, *Henry V*, Prologue, ll. 23–31.

of scenery representing a bush and addresses the actor masquerading as a lord: 'Lord Leicester, you have seduced my wife, ravished my two daughters, led astray my only son, robbed me of my wealth and burnt down my castle. I warn you, Lord Leicester: Don't take things too far!'

27. From Lessing's *Hamburg Dramaturgy*: At another, even shoddier tragedy, in which one of the main characters dropped dead in the bloom of health, a spectator asked his neighbour, 'But what on earth did she die of?' 'What of? Of the fifth act,' he replied.

28. Goethe's *Clavigo* (1774) contains the following scene:

> *The Street before the House of Gilbert. Night.*
>
> (*The house is open. Before the door stand three men clad in black mantles, holding torches. Clavigo enters, wrapt in a cloak, his sword under his arm; a servant goes before him with a torch.*)
>
> CLAVIGO. I thought I told you to avoid this street.
>
> SERVANT. We must have gone a great way round, sir, and you are in such haste. It is not far hence where Don Carlos is lodged.
>
> CLAVIGO. Torches there!
>
> SERVANT. A funeral. Come on, sir.
>
> CLAVIGO. Maria's abode! A funeral! A death-agony shudders through all my limbs. Go, ask, whom they are going to bury.
>
> SERVANT (*to the men*). Whom are you going to bury?
>
> THE MEN. Maria de Beaumarchais
>
> CLAVIGO (*sits down on a stone and covers himself in a cloak*).[13]

---

[13] Cited in William Taylor, *Historic Survey of German Poetry: Interspersed with Various Translations*, vol. 3 (London: Treuttel and Würtz, 1830), p. 305.

The story goes that at one performance featuring Moissi[14] as Clavigo, one of the men, flustered at sharing the stage with so distinguished an actor, replied to the servant's question 'Whom are you going to bury?': 'Minna von Barnhelm.'[15]

29. All these anecdotes take drama to the point of absurdity. We have already shown that drama, when defined as the representation of possibility, has an inherently subjective element. Possible is what people regard as possible—if people believe in the possibility of a miracle, then a miracle is possible for them. It is for good reason that Lessing addresses the phenomenon of the onstage miracle in the very second section of his *Hamburg Dramaturgy*. We tolerate miracles only in the physical world, Lessing says; in the moral world everything must stay its orderly course, because theatre is supposed to be the school of the moral world. This is illustrated especially by our first theatre anecdote. We can only laugh at the morality of this Job, which seems implausible to us, at the threat 'Don't take things too far,' when Lord Leicester has already taken it so far that it can go no farther. Thus Lessing does not call into question the possibility of a dramaturgical miracle, perhaps in a concession to his age, as I speculated about Aristotle. Certainly in the present day, with efforts underway to demythologize Christianity, the question of the miracle is posed much more pointedly. In our scientific age we have eliminated the miracle, removing it from the realm of the possible. What is impossible cannot be possible.

30. Here a few words on my own account. I would like to discuss my comedy *The Meteor* (1966). In dialectical fashion

14 Alexander Moissi (1879–1935): Major German-language stage actor of the early twentieth century.

15 Minna von Barnhelm: Eponymous heroine of a popular 1767 comedy by Lessing.

it poses the question of whether a man of our time who does not believe in miracles believes in a miracle when he experiences it himself: Can a present-day Lazarus believe in his own resurrection? The critical response to my comedy was instructive. It turned out that most critics didn't even take notice of Nobel Laureate Schwitters' resurrection, although it takes place several times on stage with perfect clarity. They behaved exactly like Schwitter himself, who doesn't believe in his own death either, interpreting it instead as a misdiagnosis by the doctor. Still more instructive was the attitude of the clergy. They attacked my observation that the scandal of Christianity lies in the belief in Christ's resurrection. They stressed that the scandal lies in the cross, but in so doing they merely proved that, for fear of appearing old-fashioned, they were attempting to eliminate the miracle from Christianity, making it into a petty-bourgeois ideology so innocuous as to affront no one. The cross itself has long ceased to be a scandal compared with the barbaric monstrosities often enough committed against humanity in its name. The inhumanity of the Crusades, the wars of religion, the Inquisition, as well as the wars between different nations and races, and Auschwitz, are greater scandals than the cross. Only through the resurrection does the cross become 'a stumbling block and folly',[16] not only for the Jews and the Greeks but also for the people of today. Only, it imbues the horror with meaning 'from a Christian point of view'. To see the cross by itself as a scandal is thus an effort to instal a Christianity without faith, making Christianity into a mere philosophy. In the context of these efforts *The Meteor* is rendered dialectically impossible, since it is impossible for a dead man to be resurrected. This made *The Meteor* not only a scandal for the Christians-turned-bourgeoisie, one of

16 1 Corinthians 1:23.

whose clergymen even blamed me for suggesting that God would have pardoned, of all people, an adulterer and drinker like Schwitter—as though mercy depended on irreproachable bourgeois conduct—but also a scandal for those who are not Christians but merely aesthetes. For this reason, only true Christians and true non-Christians can understand *The Meteor* on a dialectical level—the fact of the miracle is juxtaposed to the impossibility of believing in it. On the other hand, 'faith' is impossible without the individual's trust in those who testify to the miracle. In Schwitter's frenzy of death, the total individual is taken to the point of absurdity. But communism must do the same, which puts *The Meteor* in the sphere of the unique dialogue which the true Marxist Konrad Farner[17] attempts to conduct with the true Christians and which could be so productive for both positions. Well, Farner's dialogue seems to have been understood no better than my *Meteor*; Farner resigned from the Communist Party, while I was denounced by socialist aesthetes as a 'non-committed writer', though I don't wish to equate the two cases—Farner's fate is harrowing while mine is merely comical. In any event, *The Meteor* offers dramaturgical evidence that drama cannot be satisfactorily defined as the representation of the possible.

31. But first let us return to the anecdote which Lessing relates. Drama that aims to represent the possible must be based on logic if it is to eliminate the subjective element of possibility. It cannot avoid subjecting itself to the laws of nature as universalities without suffering the fate described in the *Clavigo* anecdote, in which an actor's slip of the tongue transports the astonished spectator as though by magic into a different play. Drama turns deterministic. It

17 Konrad Farner (1903–74): Swiss intellectual persecuted for his socialist views, rediscovered by the 1968 student movement.

must tell the story logically from the beginning; and as a story in the theatre must also come to a logical end, it is for logic's sake that so many people die onstage in the fifth act. This grants them not only the most radical exit but also the most imposing one. There is a second reason as well. There is a penchant for translating drama's governing law of causality, of cause and effect, into the moral sphere, to the effect that every crime must find its punishment, though admittedly the suspicion that this moral law is wishful thinking cannot be entirely dismissed. This gave rise to the bourgeois tragedy, naturalism and psychologism and ultimately (if the laws of nature are understood to include Marxism) to Marxist, socially critical, committed drama.

32. To stick to my own dramatic experiments, not out of vanity but because I know them best, the persistence of the notion that a drama must be thoroughly determinate was vividly demonstrated when several critics kept arguing that the weakness of my play *The Visit* (1956) lay in Claire Zachanassian's response when the judge asked what she did after the paternity trial which she wrongfully lost: 'I became a prostitute.' This response, the critics argued, was not imperative. Of course, Claire Zachanassian, at that time Klara Wäscher, could also have stayed in Güllen and become a maid or a factory worker. But she is characterized by the fact that she went to Hamburg and became a prostitute— the reason lies in her character. There is an internal and an external logic. It is the immanent logic of a play, not the external, that must hold true. Claire Zachanassian was faced with a choice and she chose. To try to determine even this would be to eliminate freedom.

33. What I mean by a play's immanent and external logic is also demonstrated by the *Clavigo* scene I cited. Clavigo's words 'I thought I told you to avoid this street' and the servant's reply 'We must have gone a great way round, sir, and

you are in such haste' are part of the play's external logic. Their only purpose is to explain why Clavigo passes Maria's house and to usher in the effective scene at Maria de Beaumarchais' bier. Goethe could easily have omitted these lines. On stage it is enough for an event to be immanently motivated for it to take place. It does not need to be externally motivated as well. Nonetheless, it cannot be denied that the opening lines of the scene have a certain immanent logic. It is only natural that Clavigo wishes to avoid the street leading past the house of his betrayed beloved. In drama, the difference between immanent and external logic often lies in mere nuances, in the parts of a picture which we merely sketch and those which we aim to render in detail. To determine everything would be to detail everything.

34. What is true of a person's freedom of choice, to decide one way or the other, is also true of coincidence. Looking closely, one finds that even the most determinate drama cannot manage without coincidence. The coincidence is the unforeseeable. For the ancients it took the form of fate. Even coincidence, if properly used, belongs to a play's immanent, not external, logic. Of course it is a coincidence that the assessor Walter shows up to review Judge Adam's performance at the very moment when Adam must sit in judgement over himself; he could just as well have appeared a day later.[18] But his fateful appearance at an awkward moment belongs to the immanent rather than the external logic of the play.

35. But a certain uneasiness remains as we examine the relationship between drama and possibility—drama as an image of possibility comes into conflict with reality; in aiming to

18 Reference to *The Broken Jug* (1808), a comedy by Heinrich von Kleist. Judge Adam must sit in judgement over a crime (the breaking of the jug) of which he himself is secretly guilty.

represent only the possible and not the real, it only appears to be imperative, for there are many possibilities, not just one, whereas there is only one reality—the possibility which does become real. Whether or not it wants to, the drama of possibility acts as though it were real. It is precisely this acting 'as though possibility were reality' which Max Frisch opposes. 'I am merely observing,' he wrote to Walter Höllerer,[19]

> that as a playwright I can no longer use a certain dramaturgy I have learnt. I have dubbed it the dramaturgy of providence, the dramaturgy of peripeteia. You're right, that's a vague label which could mean many things: ancient drama with its divine providence, psychological drama, ultimately even Brecht, though instead of having the gods prevail he reveals the imperatives of the social system and presents his plots in terms of this inevitability. In any case, what I mean is a dramaturgy that always tries to create the impression that a plot could have unfolded only thus and not otherwise, that is, it admits as credible only what is imperative in the sense of causality; it has no desire or ability to render coincidence plausible. But that is exactly what occupies me right now, the issue of the arbitrary nature of every story. A plot, I believe, can never mean that the same   characters in the same environment couldn't also have given rise to a completely different plot, a different game than the one which did become the story, biography or world history . . . We know that things happen only if they are possible, but a   thousand equally possible things do not happen,   and everything could always take a completely different course. This we know but it

---

19 Walter Höllerer (1922–2003): German writer and literary critic.

does not become apparent as long as only one course of events is shown on stage (as in reality). What of the equally possible variants? Each course of events on stage, excluding all other courses of events by the very fact of its occurrence, is ultimately ascribed a meaning it does not deserve; the impression is of inevitability, fate, providence. Things performed always have a propensity to meaning which things lived do not. Where do you see the open doors?[20]

36. This question which Frisch asks of drama must of course be taken seriously. The only issue is whether it is not in fact a specious question.

37. *Drama and Probability.* In drama, as in other spheres of thought, there is always the question of whether one is working with the appropriate mental tools. So far we have been operating with the terms reality, possibility and impossibility. What is real is the possibility that has been realized; the possibility is the possibility that could be realized. Impossibility remains impossible because it can't be realized. Possibility and impossibility are mutually exclusive. Now we must consider how dramaturgy would look if different terms were used, for example, those of the probable and the improbable. They have a different relationship to reality—both the improbable and the probable can become real. The probable will more probably become real than the improbable, but dialectically the two terms are not mutually exclusive, as the terms possibility and impossibility are. If it's possible that it will rain tomorrow, it can rain tomorrow; if it's impossible, it can't rain. If it's probable that it will rain tomorrow, it can

20 Max Frisch, *Dramaturgisches: Ein Briefwechsel mit Walter Höllerer* (Dramaturgy: Correspondence with Walter Höllerer) (Berlin: Literarisches Colloquium Berlin, 1969), p. 8.

rain tomorrow; if it's improbable, it can rain nonetheless.

38. *For Example, An Accident.* One May morning in 1959 I found myself unable to write. Loath to agonize at my desk, I decided to take a drive into the blue. Passing through Murten I ended up at an inn in Gruyere, not far from Lake Geneva, where I ate lunch. Though I had meant to return home, I was in such a good mood following the excellent trout that I decided to drive to the Valais to stock up on wine. Hot spring weather. I had a fast car but drove at a leisurely pace, I had time. I took a wrong turn in Vevey, got stuck behind a convoy of trucks which I managed to pass after Aigle, then headed towards Bex. Before me lay a slight elevation from the top of which I could see far down the road. It ran straight, then made a wide curve to the right. A truck filled with workers trundled along three hundred yards ahead of me, and a car approached on the distant, open curve. I wondered briefly whether to pass the truck— my car was fast enough—but decided to be careful, slowing down and driving along behind the truck filled with workers, intending to let past the car which I had seen approaching from a distance. Unexpectedly, the truck in front of me turned right onto a dirt road leading to a construction site. That was when the accident happened. In my rear-view mirror I saw a rapidly approaching car which clearly hadn't noticed the car coming in the other direction until the truck made its turn. The two cars collided abreast of me, grazing my car and hurling it across the road into the field where it came to a stop, upright. Fortunately, I had my seatbelt on. A crash, a shattering of glass, deathly silence. Then cries, lots of blood, two blood-soaked men slogging away at each other, a total of five people seriously injured. I sat unscathed in my car. People had suddenly appeared all around. I didn't move. The right side of my car was crushed. I sat, no longer looking at the road, where a woman was screaming appallingly. I'd escaped once again. Apathetically I sat behind the steering wheel, unable to feel or intervene, offer assistance; it must have been the shock. But there was something that especially bothered me, something which jarred with the event and which I only hit upon after minutes had passed—through all the screams of the wounded, my car radio was playing a Haydn symphony.

39. *Dramaturgy of This Accident.* Viewed dramaturgically, at first glance the accident consists of nothing but coincidences. Of course I can identify the chain of coincidences only from my perspective: I could have stayed home, I could have spent more or less time eating, I might not have driven to the Valais at all, I might have driven slower or faster, I needn't have taken a wrong turn in Vevey, etc. A similar chain of coincidences could be established for the other cars involved in the accident. If one selects a certain random point in time before the accident, between this point in time and the accident more or fewer coincidences have to take place to ensure that the accident occurs. The closer the point in time is to the accident, the more probable it is that the accident will come to pass; the further back in time, the more improbable. And so we can venture the definition that reality is the improbability that has occurred.

40. Of course, this does not suspend causality. I can regard each coincidence as both the effect of a new cause and as the cause of a new effect. Seen backwards from the accident, one single chain of causation leads to it—though from a point in time three hours before the accident it is highly improbable that three particular cars will collide between Aigle and Bex, from the point of time of the accident it is, in retrospect, inevitable, because one fact meshes with the other.

41. Regarding the 'dramaturgy of coincidence' which Frisch cites. In his play *Biography* (1968), which is based on his 'dramaturgy', he aims to show that each event could also have unfolded differently, that different results are also conceivable, that each person's biography is a highly problematic aggregate of incidents that are anything but imperative. Of course he is right about that. The only question is whether his dramaturgy doesn't collide with the notion of reality. The infernal thing about reality is that it comes true, that it plays out as it plays out, that although it is improbable it is causal. We are subjected to this reality and no other. Thus, strictly speaking, Frisch's *Biography* is a fairy-tale play. Not to denigrate fairy-tale plays, though. Precisely because they are fairy-tale plays, they are able to convey an analysis of our reality.

42. The danger of contemporary writing is that you pursue the 'as if' without really pursuing it. You act as if you're improvising but in fact the improvisation is rehearsed and refined. You act as if the author were no longer the omniscient Good Lord who knows everything about a given story, but in fact you're still the Good Lord after all. The more precisely I try to define an art, the more cramped is the cage in which it confines me. This is especially true of dramaturgy. Drama in which possibility appears as reality is just as confining as Frisch's proposal that dramaturgy should pass off reality as possibility. Whether I render an event as coincidental or causal is not a dialectical contradiction; rather, these are merely two possible ways to represent the event. Hence my proposal to operate more with the terms 'probable' and 'improbable', since it makes no difference whether I tell a probable or an improbable story. In both cases I describe reality by means of fiction, I act as though reality could be described using fiction—in fact there is no other way to describe it.

43. *Drama as Fiction.* If, as Aristotle has it, the historian and the dramatist differ in the fact that one tells what has happened while the other tells what could happen, I would like to define the task of the dramatist as describing what would probably happen if, improbably enough, some specific thing occurred. What happens improbably enough is the dramatic incident the dramatist has chosen; what probably happens is the dramatic development of this chosen event. Dramaturgy would then consist in the immanent critique of what the author allows to happen once he has established his fiction. The critique would not pose such questions as whether it is permissible, as in Frisch's *Biography*, to invent a situation in which someone is allowed to relive his life; rather, it would have to determine whether the author had properly executed his fiction. The critique would have to think through what probably happens and not what improbably happens. In Frisch's *Biography*, the game leads dramaturgically to a sequence of variations. I would have to consider whether these variations had been executed properly or faultily,   or whether they could have been exercised still better. For example, when Kürmann knows that he meets the woman with whom he later has an unhappy marriage at a party he throws to celebrate his appointment as professor, and we are then shown in different variations that the party, if it takes place, will inevitably lead to an unhappy marriage, one must ask whether it makes sense for Kürmann to decide to become a communist just so he can't become a professor, whether   it wouldn't be more obvious simply not to throw a party, whether here the author isn't telling us what would happen improbably enough if something improbable occurred.

44. Regarding the supposition that drama consists in establishing dramatic fictions: Someone who establishes a fiction is consciously acting as if. Frisch consciously acts as if it were possible to relive one's life. In *The Meteor* I consciously act as if a person could repeatedly rise from the dead. Different things are achieved here. With his 'as if', Frisch is able to analyse a life outside the rigid chain of causation which this life would acquire if seen in the retrospective sense of what has been. In the case of *The Meteor* I am able to represent the death wish—in his constant belief that he is dying, Schwitter shoots through society as a meteor shoots through the atmosphere. He becomes the absolute loner, one who is always right because he is dying and, above all, is always allowed to be right because no one dares to contradict a dying man. By surrendering completely to his death drive, he surrenders just as completely to his drive for power.

45. *The Worst Possible Turn.* The dramaturgy of the accident indicated the following: an accident is initially improbable, growing more and more probable over the course of time until it becomes reality—the chain of circumstances, coincidences, etc., has taken the worst possible turn. It is possible for me to survive an accident with only a scratch, but this scratch still represents the worst possible turn, because the worst possible turn represents the reality, that is, the accident as it happened and not as it could have happened. If I establish a fiction, I am not reproducing reality. Reality occurs, playing out in the 'ontological' realm, fiction in the logical. Thus, mentally I must make my fiction take the worst possible turn, I must describe the fatal accident. Only then does my mental fiction acquire an 'existential' justification. As human beings, we are threatened by the worst possibilities on an existential level as well, not only by the atom bomb but also by the worst possible social order, by the worst possible marriage, etc. By making a dramatic fiction take the worst possible turn, I achieve, via a peculiarly negative detour, ethicality—the confrontation of a mental fiction with the existential. Only then, for example, is Kürmann's decision to join the Communist Party justified—it is the worst possible turn. Not because Kürmann joins the Communist Party but because he joins the Communist

Party to avoid having to throw a party later on, that is, to avoid having to break a bourgeois taboo—people who become professors have to throw parties. Thus Frisch, in his *Biography*, chooses the worst possible person as his titular hero—the philistine. Frisch's *Biography* is the comedy of the philistine, though it is not always understood as such.

46. *The Significance of Drama as Fiction.* In his *The Philosophy of As If* (1911), Hans Vaihinger[21] asked how it is that we are able to achieve the right thing on the basis of consciously false notions. From a dramaturgical perspective I would like to shift this question to ask how it is that we are able to describe reality on the basis of consciously invented notions. Now, I am not a philosopher, and so I am unable to solve this question as it deserves to be solved. I can only offer some speculations. At the same time, I don't want to equate the two questions. A fiction of mathematics or physics is different than an artistic one. A fiction of physics strikes me as a conscious thought technique with which I set a sort of trap for reality, thus eliciting an answer from it, but one which I can interpret only in terms of physics; artistic fictions strike me as thought techniques that aim at establishing apparent realities. While a fiction of physics interrogates reality, the artistic fiction artificially creates reality, an artificial counter-reality to reality as it is, mirroring reality as it is. Whereas in the fiction of physics everything lies in the consciously precise formulation of the question, whose cunningness consists of its 'as if', and whereas one achieves thereby nothing but an answer tricked out of reality, namely a physical one, the answer which an artistic fiction gives depends a lot on the perspective from which I view the mirror. Depending on my position, a mirror shows me this or that part of reality as reflected in it. Whereas the fiction of

21 Hans Vaihinger (1852–1933): German philosopher.

physics offers the possibility of insight into the physical world, the artistic fiction offers many insights, by no means of purely artistic nature. Whereas one engages our physical knowledge of the world, the other engages our general experiences with the world. Knowledge and empiricism are not the same. Art is no more philosophy than is physics but both are material for philosophy. The more drama dares to provide nothing but material for philosophy, the better it fulfils its purpose in the overall spectrum of human thought. I believe it is an error of contemporary drama that it so often seeks to be both, drama and philosophy, for then it becomes neither, and perhaps the reason we lack a major philosophy today is that everyone is trying to pursue one.

ASPECTS OF DRAMATURGICAL THINKING

FRAGMENT

1964

On Narration. In the broadest sense, dramaturgy attempts to establish a theory of a certain technique of narration. Drama, as the object of dramaturgy, can thus be traced back to the epic. Narration requires a narrator, the material that is narrated and the listener (or reader) to whom the narrative is addressed. The narrator can depict the material (the found or invented object) from within and from without, he can convey the thoughts, emotions and speech of his characters as well as depict the overall context within which they move, etc.—there is nothing that cannot be depicted. Narration is a subjective art; as a narrator (as a subject, as a writer, as an 'I') the epicist has absolute control over his material. The epic displays two tendencies: one that aspires from the subjective to the apparently objective (apparently—even with the strictest objectivity it is the narrator, the writer who tells the story, and of course this also holds for the dramatist); and one that holds fast to the subjective, indeed sees it as the special chance narration offers. The epic becomes an opportunity for the writer to present himself, to justify himself, turning into confessional and diary literature or, as with Jean Paul,[1] into a narrative technique whereby the 'I' unhesitatingly intervenes in the story. The

---

1 Jean Paul (1763–1825): German Romantic writer.

tendency towards the apparently objective begins with the narrating I of writers such as Proust or Frisch who hovers between fiction and reality and plays with this contradiction (*Gantenbein*[2]), moving from Kafka's stylized I (K.) to the fictitious I's of a Defoe or Swift, proceeding from fictitious narrators (rather than telling the story himself, the narrator seems to be passing along someone else's story) to apparently objective narration that eschews the fiction of a narrator.

On Drama. Leaving aside the fact that radio plays, television and film have created new possibilities, the narrative technique of dramatic art can be defined by the fact that there is no I as the point of departure. The stage knows no I. If a narrator appears, or if a dramatist hits on the notion of putting himself on stage, like the ancient comic playwright Cratinus, for the viewer this narrator, or Cratinus, is not an I but an Other. Drama objectifies the material, thrusts it onto the stage. The dramatist no longer has absolute control over the material. He is limited by the stage. Not everything can be shown on stage. The dramatist cannot narrate directly from within but only indirectly via the stage. He is forced to describe his creations from outside through their speech, actions and sufferings. He writes roles. The art of drama requires the art of acting (only in rhetorical drama can the actor's relationship to the text be roughly compared with the musical performer's relationship to the score). There is no viable dramaturgy that does not take the stage into account. (Kafka dramatizations illustrate the lacking I—the adapters were forced to show Kafka's stylized I [K.] from outside, with K. as the stage hero. Kafka depicts K. from within and without; K.'s conversations, for example, are the result of complex mental deliberations. Theoretically, the best way to

2 *Gantenbein* (1964): Novel by Max Frisch.

dramatize Kafka would be through film and without ever showing K.; the camera would be K.'s eyes, as it were, the audience would see everything from K.'s perspective, supplemented in part by K.'s voiceover monologues, in part by K.'s conversations with a visible interlocutor.)

Dramaturgy in Terms of Objective. That formal pathos must be justified is, of course, a universal dramaturgical law. On its basis one can question even the German classics— Friedrich Schiller, for example: Is his pathos, his iambic language justified by the action? He instinctively wrote *The Robbers* (1781) in prose, achieving what are probably his most poetic effects; later, with Weimarian artistic judgement, he used iambs, though 'dragged down' to prose again and again, 'as declamation does everything to destroy the structure of the verses'.[3] Unfortunately he withstood the temptation but his distrust remained and propelled him in a strange direction. Though he believed that '[b]y the introduction of a metrical dialogue an important progress has been made towards the poetical tragedy',[4] with his keen dramaturgical sense he could not overlook the contradiction in which his iambic language had ensnared him.

> All the externals of a theatrical representation are opposed to this notion [of the actual]; all is merely a symbol of the real. The day itself in a theatre is an artificial one; the metrical dialogue is itself ideal; yet the conduct of the play must forsooth be real, and the general effect sacrificed to a part. Thus the French, who have utterly misconceived the spirit of

3 Letter from Friedrich Schiller to Gottfried Körner, 5 October 1801.

4 This and the following quotes are from Friedrich Schiller, *The Bride of Messina, and On the Use of the Chorus in Tragedy* (A. Lodge trans.). Available at: http://www.gutenberg.org/files/6793/6793-h/6793-h.htm (last accessed on 23 April 2013).

the ancients, adopted on their stage the unities of
time and place in the most common and empirical
sense; as though there were any place but the
bare ideal one, or any other time than the mere
sequence of the incidents.

This passage from his foreword to *The Bride of Messina*
(1803) is not just aimed at the French. Schiller himself, by
drawing on historical material for his verse plays, depicted
real actions and now felt that his metrical language was no
longer justified by the material. History remained history,
that which had occurred and not that which could have
occurred. His unease was aggravated by the belief that theatre without symbolic value was something base, a mere
entertainment, a delusion:

> To string together at will fantastical images is not to
> travel into the realm of the ideal; and the imitative
> reproduction of the actual cannot be called the rep-
> resentation of nature. Both requisites stand so little
> in contradiction to each other that they are rather
> one and the same thing; that art is only true inso-
> much as it altogether forsakes the actual, and
> becomes purely ideal. [. . .] The introduction of the
> chorus would be the last and decisive step; and if it
> only served this end, namely, to declare open and
> honourable warfare against naturalism in art, it
> would be for us a living wall which tragedy had
> drawn around herself, to guard her from contact
> with the world of reality, and maintain her own
> ideal soil, her poetical freedom. [. . .] The old
> tragedy, which at first only concerned itself with
> gods, heroes and kings introduced the chorus as an
> essential accompaniment. The poets found it in
> nature, and for that reason employed it. The actions
> and fates of the heroes and kings are public in and

of themselves, and were still more so in primitive times. [. . .] The modern poet no longer finds the chorus in nature; he must needs create and introduce it poetically; that is, he must resolve on such an adaption of his story as will admit of its retrocession to those primitive times and to that simple form of life. The chorus thus renders more substantial service to the modern dramatist than to the old poet—and for this reason, that it transforms the commonplace actual world into the old poetical one; that it enables him to dispense with all that is repugnant to poetry, and conducts him back to the most simple, original, and genuine motives of action. The palaces of kings are in these days closed—courts of justice have been transferred from the gates of cities to the interior of buildings; writing has narrowed the province of speech; the people itself—the sensibly living mass—when it does not operate as brute force, has become a part of the civil polity, and thereby an abstract idea in our minds; the deities have returned within the bosoms of mankind. The poet must reopen the palaces—he must place courts of justice beneath the canopy of heaven—restore the gods, reproduce every extreme which the artificial frame of actual life has abolished—throw aside every factitious influence on the mind or condition of man which impedes the manifestation of his inward nature and primitive character, as the statuary rejects modern costume: —and of all external circumstances adopts nothing but what is palpable in the highest of forms—that of humanity.

But the tragedy with choruses was a failure, and Schiller's doubts about the justification of metrical language were forgotten along with this experiment. In the accepted dramaturgical view, *Wallenstein* (1799) is the greatest achievement of German drama, a work in which the language nearly destroys the material—the Thirty Years War comes to life not in Schiller's iambic soldiers but in the prose of Mother Courage. Schiller's scepticism belatedly carried the day. Brecht's epic theatre has made it easier to understand Schiller's revolutionary foreword. Schiller was the first to suspect that tragic poets could no longer directly depict the present day, and tried to make it depictable by means of the chorus which 'exercises a purifying influence on tragic poetry, insomuch as it keeps reflection apart from the incidents'. Schiller demanded of the theatre a consciously artificial world, that is, a defamiliarized one—man is to recognize himself not in a likeness but in an ideal prototype, and 'acknowledge on the stage that moral government of the world which he fails to discover in real life'. If the objective of tragedy lies in its function as a moral institution, Schiller's autonomous theatrical world must be discussed in terms of its objective, otherwise it becomes ambiguous: '[The chorus] forsakes the contracted sphere of the incidents to dilate itself over the past and the future, over distant times and nations, and general humanity, to deduce the grand results of life, and pronounce the lessons of wisdom.' Brecht's dramaturgical concept has much in common with Schiller's. His idealism has more tactical precision, it is political but no less rigorous. Both think dialectically. Schiller, for example, distinguishes his chorus dialectically from that of the ancients. Schiller's present is no longer naive; he lives in a conscious age and Brecht endeavours to write for a scientific age. For Brecht, too, the present cannot be depicted directly—except 'when it is described as capable of change'. The world can be brought to the stage only by the recipe of change, in conjunction with an idea and commentated on the basis of this idea. His drama is illustrative; its task is to illustrate the idea (the message, the problem, i.e. human society's capacity for change and the means thereto) and thus infuse drama with the awareness of the class struggle. What Schiller intended with the chorus, the separation of reflection and action, Brecht achieved with the song—that is, with an infinitely more popular genre—as well as with brief interpolated texts, with instructions to the actors or even with an actual chorus. But he puts dramaturgy in a quandary by asking about drama's objective, a question that had already occupied Aristotle with fateful consequences:

> And the catharsis of which Aristotle writes— cleansing by fear and pity, or from fear and pity—is a purification which is performed not only in a pleasurable way, but precisely for the purpose of pleasure. To ask or to accept more of the theatre is to set one's own mark too low. Even when people speak of higher and lower degrees of pleasure, art stares impassively back at them; for it wishes to fly high and low and to be left in peace, so long as it can give pleasure to people.[5]

Brecht's axiom is difficult to contradict. An art's objective is always a difficult matter. Here two spheres meet that can never fully merge—the particular and the general. An answer can never come from both at once. Brecht resolutely sides with the general, answering from the standpoint of society. He admits to what others have more or less admitted, though they did so bashfully, adding a few idealistic objectives. When the bashfulness is dropped, the ideals are dropped as well. '"Theatre" consists in this: in making live representations of reported or invented happenings between human beings and doing so with a view to

5 Brecht, 'A Short Organum for the Theatre', p. 181.

entertainment'—by defining drama thus, Brecht defines his dramaturgy by the general, by society, and consequently seeks to identify the pleasures of the scientific age, which can no longer be our enjoyments from a non-scientific age; 'Our whole way of appreciation is starting to get out of date.'[6] The scientific age demands that we enjoy a theatre that is not merely imitative, like Aristotelian theatre, but also critical. 'But if the theatre be made instrumental towards higher objects, the diversion, of the spectator will not be increased, but ennobled. It will be a diversion, but a poetical one. All art is dedicated to pleasure, and there can be no higher and worthier end than to make men happy. The true art is that which provides the highest degree of pleasure; and this consists in the abandonment of the spirit to the free play of all its faculties.' Those are Schiller's words. Brecht: 'The theatre of the scientific age is in a position to make dialectics into a source of enjoyment. The unexpectedness of logically progressive or zigzag development, the instability of every circumstance, the joke of contradiction and so forth, all these are ways of enjoying the liveliness of men, things and processes, and they heighten both our capacity for life and our pleasure in it. Every art contributes to the greatest art of all, the art of living.'[7] Every enjoyment pre-supposes someone capable of enjoying. In the end, however, both Schiller and Brecht jump back from the general to the particular. Brecht conceptualizes the person of the scientific age. And it is this person who will give him the answer, inde-pendent of the justified or unjustified objections that could be made against his dramaturgy. The question is not only whether Brecht has correctly conceptualized this person and thus this person's society, and whether he even conceptual-

6 Ibid., p. 183.
7 Ibid., p. 277.

izes science correctly, but also whether this person, if Brecht's conception stands, wants the enjoyment which Brecht proposes to him, one now enjoyed mainly by the children of a not-yet-scientific age. Perhaps what this person wants is uncommentated, non-deliberate theatre, so as to draw his own conclusions, perhaps sentiment, emotions, romanticism, perhaps kitsch, perhaps illusions, perhaps heroism, chivalric tales of cosmonauts, perhaps prayers, perhaps curses, perhaps anarchy. 'But science and art meet on this ground, that both are there to make men's life easier, the one setting out to maintain, the other to entertain us.'[8] The iron face of art is mute, and the Janus head of science smiles two-faced. What Brecht takes for its objectives may be nothing but its financing methods. That art can also be entertainment may merely be its maintenance.

Dramaturgy in Terms of the Individual. Whereas Brecht established his own dramaturgy, thus giving critics the opportunity to praise him and know exactly why they are doing so, much remains unclear, dramaturgically speaking, about absurd theatre, and the term seems more absurd than the plays themselves. Theatre = theatre. Theatre can only be theatre. This identity theorem is Eugene Ionesco's contribution to dramaturgy. He was reacting against the fact that for others theatre meant 'ideology, allegory, politics, lectures, essays or literature',[9] which he found just as perverse as insisting that music should be archaeology or painting physics or mathematics. Besides—a key demand of his dramaturgy —he argued that theatre must be freed of all that is not pure theatre, taking his cue from modern painting which

---

8 Ibid., p. 185.

9 Eugene Ionesco, 'Discovering the Theatre' (1959) in Robert Willoughby Corrigan (ed.), *Theatre in the Twentieth Century* (New York: Grove Press, 1963), pp. 77–93; here, p. 91.

attempted nothing other than to free itself from what is not painting, from literature, from anecdote, history and photography. Yet Ionesco's statement leads to a contradiction. The theatre is the place where something is shown, where something is performed. A murder in the theatre is an acted murder. Theatre always signifies something else—that which is represented through the theatre. Theatre is not the world, it signifies the world, be it capable of change or merely of restructuring; if theatre meant nothing but theatre, it would be meaningless. Theatre = theatre. Theatre is never reality but acted reality (thus theatre can never prove anything but at most illustrate it, as is the case with didactic plays), never illusion but acted illusion. But that is also why theatre can be used as an instrument for ideology, allegory, politics, etc.; as a stage for shows, theatre by its very nature is an opportunity for the most diverse and contradictory things; by its nature it lets itself be prostituted; it itself, and its terms, offer no way to restrict these possibilities; there is nothing to be inferred from the identity theorem, not even a dramaturgy. Ionesco's theorem must be understood as a polemic. It is aimed against naturalism. While Brecht (and with him expressionism) had already tried to establish a non-naturalistic theatre not by abolishing illusion—without illusion no theatre is possible—but by rendering it recognizable as such, Ionesco tried to fall back on purely theatrical elements. He postulated:

> It was necessary not to hide the strings, but to make them even more visible, deliberately evident, to go all the way in the grotesque, in caricature, beyond the pale irony of witty drawing room comedies. Not drawing room comedies, but farce, an extreme burlesque exaggeration. Humor, yes, but with the methods of burlesque. A hard comedy, without

10 Ibid., p. 85.

> finesse, excessive. No dramatic comedies either.
> But a return to the intolerable. Push everything to
> a state of paroxysm, there where the sources of
> tragedy lie. Create a theatre of violence: violently
> comic, violently tragic.[10]

This dramaturgy could be developed from the question of what theatre as such, primal theatre, actually is—from a question that has already been posed historically and that has led to cultic theatre, to demonic invocations, mysteries, etc. But the disadvantage of these inquiries was that they strayed into other cultural epochs and thus bore no fruits for the present. When one asks the question ahistorically, seeking an immediate, unliterary primal theatre in the present, one finds the clown. Here the actor has just one function—to depict a person one can't help laughing at, the original unlucky devil who goes about everything ineptly, on whom the dead objects take their revenge. This ancient theatre and circus character (Harlequin) has been given new life by Chaplin and influences popular comedians such as Valentin time and again. The 'drama' of the clown develops out of the situation and works with situation comedy, props become crucial, even taking on a life of their own, dialogue hopelessly confuses the situation rather than straightening it out, etc. What Beckett and Ionesco send onto the stage are clowns without masks. In these characters, the hero's inexorable social decline from mythical demigod to kings and noblemen, the bourgeois hero and Baal reaches its culmination. Büchner's[11] Andres and Woyzeck live on in Beckett's Vladimir and Estragon, and one seems to find Sternheim's[12]

---

11 Georg Büchner (1813–37): German dramatist and poet, famous for his work *Woyzeck* (1837).

12 Carl Sternheim (1878–1942): German dramatist and short-story writer, major figure of German expressionism.

philistines in Ionesco's creations, albeit dodgier, still more shadowy, more nameless, more bottom-dwelling, the last of men in the last of situations, parallel phenomena to the concept of the individual, which, arisen from the all-powerful I of idealism and romanticism and conceived in opposition to its boundlessness, denotes the isolated, cast-out person, the person who with his kind no longer forms a family, a people, an organism, but merely a mass, who is left at the mercy of existence, nothingness (or God), the moment, fear and loneliness or however one calls the stations of the tunnel of horror through which existentialism sends humanity careering. The individual appears not only reduced to sheer existence but also divested of character, discharged from all social functions; seen from within, he is the very paragon of interiority and thus an objectified I which, costumed as a clown, now enters the stage that knows no I—once again a dramaturgical law has been outsmarted. Ionesco seems to allude to this

> When Richard II, fallen from power, is alone imprisoned in his cell, it is not Richard II that I see, but all the fallen kings of the earth; and not only all the fallen kings, but also our beliefs, our values, our desacralized truths, corrupted, worn out, our civilizations which disappear, our destiny. When Richard II dies, it is what I hold most dear that I see die; it is I who die with Richard II.[13]

13 Ibid., p. 89.

AUTHOR'S NOTE: For our purposes, the example of Richard II is perhaps an unfortunate choice on Ionesco's part. Richard II is not an 'individual'; he remains a character, and thus a hero. A hero—however down and out—emerges with the plot. The reduction of the person to the 'individual' corresponds to the reduction of the plot to the situation. In this respect, Beckett is more reliable for the theoretician—he is one single repetition of one last possible situation, and the fact that he

For Ionesco, Richard II is an 'individual', an 'I'. For the individual the world may be absurd, unbearable. The theatre that registers this possibility is not. Seismographs are not absurd either.

constantly repeats himself is all that makes him believable. By contrast, Ionesco ends up contradicting the dramaturgy that we call his as soon as he switches from situation to plot, as soon as he writes an evening-length play. Behringer is no longer an individual, he is already a hero again—a decent person. Ionesco runs into difficulties similar to Sartre's, albeit for the opposite reasons—Ionesco campaigns against all ideologies while Sartre campaigns for one, though without accepting himself as a hardliner (today this sort of acceptance is more impossible than ever: the Party writes crooked on straight lines); Sartre tries to use his opponent to defeat his enemies. Assuming that the nineteenth century has bequeathed us, apart from science, two intellectual stances which cannot be brought into alignment—dialectical materialism, conceived on the basis of the general, and existentialism (to which theories of cognition also ultimately lead), conceived on the basis of the I—then Sartre is trying to be a Marxist on the basis of existentialism. His *No Exit* (1944) launched the 'theatre of the absurd', with four 'individuals' who find themselves in Hell. Later, his political committedness forced him to use heroes once again to anchor his dramaturgy. The 'individual' is no more a reality than is a clown. He is a conception, a notion of conscious or unconscious existentialism, while a 'hero' is still included in the furniture which social realism took with it from the nice bourgeois apartment. The bourgeois furnishings of Marxism can also be seen in the fact that the Politburo and the bourgeoisie agree on matters of taste— they both demand positive heroes. Finally—as long as we are making notes—concerning the position of my highly personal dramaturgy within these dramaturgical systems, I hope that I have now confused this position to such an extent that those critics who have threatened to rethink me may not be able to keep up with me, but may at least have been presented with far better weapons for their hatchet jobs. Anyone with a modicum of self-love will ensure that his critics don't use dum-dum bullets. Note well: Do not reveal your dramaturgy, otherwise you will be forced to hold to it one day.

Language = language. We instinctively locate language between music and painting—it moves forward in time, has melody and rhythm, is capable of evoking precise images and ideas, concepts, allusions to real, possible, impossible things. Today, the demands which Ionesco

Dramaturgy in Terms of the Material (Draft). If there exists a dramaturgy in terms of objective (and thus of the idea), there must also exist a dramaturgy in terms of material, a

placed on theatre are also being placed on language. Writers are accused of failing to keep up with developments in music and painting. But while music and painting are in fact capable of approaching pure form and having only themselves as their content, the potential of language to be pure language, language as such, is dubious. What is true of theatre is also true in a certain sense of language—it is not reality but represents it, characterizes it, alludes to it, expresses it. The relationship of language to reality is anything but unambiguous, the relation of concept to reality justifiably poses one of the main problems of philosophy and physics. Language as such would be content-free, yet the adventure of language lies in the tension between language and what it signifies. Writing is more than a mere preoccupation with language, for language derives its value not from itself but from its object, that which it articulates. But the proclivity towards the stylistic, to 'pure language', has seized not only the critics who wield grammar like a guillotine, arguing that language alone is examinable, unsuspecting that true language and true style can be more cryptic, more hidden and more ungrammatical than they think, but also many writers, who can barely write for sheer style. The content of language consists of thoughts;. one works on thoughts, not on language; one works on thoughts through language. Great language is precise by its content, not by itself. Those who try to work with language alone, taking language as mere material and thus seeking their content in it, become imprecise. When everything is possible, there are no criteria left—in the realm of absolute freedom nothing matters. Then writers merely exploit language's autonomous laws, letting it run rampant, playing with associations, working with coincidences. They weave nets in the hope of capturing reality but reality snarls itself in such webs only on serendipitous occasions (though admittedly those are great moments). Those who wish to forge ahead into virgin linguistic territory (as almost everyone claims these days) must aim not at language, but at new content—new contexts, new conflicts, problems, the newly thought. Otherwise they will only conquer the domains hedged in by public morality or loot the cache of concepts from which today's world washes up flotsam at their feet every day, scraps of language from domains among which no more than a vague understanding is now possible, the complexity of the new subject areas being too vast.

practical dramaturgy, usually deployed instinctively when writing a play or when directing (which comes closest to writing) but also when acting in existing plays or thinking them through from a dramaturgical point of view (the grand attempt—Lessing); a dramaturgy that underlies all other dramaturgies, for even if one aims to render a material usable for an idea, one must always think and conceptualize in terms of the material. The method of this dramaturgy—one must investigate the material to determine its dramaturgical possibilities; reflecting on existing plays, one must always begin by thinking with, not against the author, playing and overseeing his part and no other (a rule of fair play). Dramaturgy in terms of the material thinks through the stage possibilities of a material; its main concern is how to depict a certain material on a certain stage. However, the criterion that makes a masterpiece a masterpiece lies outside dramaturgy which cannot verify the worth or worthlessness of an art; a dramaturgy in terms of material is not an aesthetic but an empirical compilation of the rules and tricks that make up a craft. Nonetheless, the dramaturgy in terms of material is not merely an auxiliary dramaturgy, in the sense, for example, of the dramaturgical skill that is understood to underlie every dramatic art. It is also the dramaturgy of those dramatists who see the material itself as the objective subject of dramatic art which they transform into a symbol of reality (not an allegory), into a parable which by nature is not clear but ambiguous, which poses not one problem but several. Schiller provides an example of this as well. After the theoretical venture of *The Bride of Messina*, he turned to myth, writing *William Tell* (1804) (and it is surely no coincidence that in his clumsy but explosive *The Deputy*, Hochhuth, the last of Schiller's heirs, addresses the last myth that still survives, that of the infallible pope whom the Catholic Church cannot pronounce guilty because he cannot be guilty). Swiss national drama is based on Schiller's grandest material. Here he found the poetic, ideal plot which justified his metrical, pathos-filled language. *William Tell* is a pageant, especially suited for open-air theatres and amateur actors; when they speak this language, it sounds truly naive, one stops wondering why mountain farmers are speaking in iambs; and yet the play is revolutionary—the true agent is the collective. Tell does not need a chorus. The collective as agent was forced upon Schiller not by an idea but by the material. This makes the material crucial, the creativity which discovers or creates the material, the technique of inventing material (meaning that dramaturgy ought to begin with the material, preferably operating with examples). Crucial—the object determines the actions of the subject who must choose (how one chooses characterizes the dramatist) between different possibilities provided by the object (by the material). Writing becomes obedience to the material. Distinguishing between conflict and problem.

1952

I am concerned here with establishing that one of the crucial differences between the art of Aristophanes and that of Sophocles, for example, lies in its strokes of creativity, one of the key features of ancient Attic comedy. I don't mean to say that the tragic playwrights of antiquity had no creative notions, as is the case today, but their unparalleled artistry lay in the fact that they needed none. That is a difference.

A prerequisite for poetic pathos on the stage is a familiar material. This peculiar circumstance is much more important than one might think at first glance. I wouldn't necessarily have wanted to see the tragedy by Agathon which, according to Aristotle, was the first with an invented plot. *The Bride of Messina* is Schiller's most dubious work because it is his invention, and Goethe's infinitely more poetic *The Natural Daughter* (1803) suffers greatly for the same reason. Yet Aristophanes lives from creativity, *is* creativity, and, in this respect, an oddity among Greek artists. His materials are not myths, like those of the tragic playwrights, but invented plots, set not in the past but in the present. In *The Acharnians*, an Attic farmer makes a private peace with the Spartans in the midst of the Peloponnesian War; in another of his comedies, the birds establish a realm between heaven and earth, forcing humans and gods to capitulate; in *Peace*, a gian beetle is ridden to the heavens to bring back Peace, a whore, to humanity; in *Lysistrata*, the Greek women use a simple but effective means to end the war between their men. What all these proceedings have in common is very much the stroke of creativity; they live from this creativity, are made possible by it alone. These are creative notions that strike the world like projectiles (to use an image) which reshape the present into comedy by gouging out a crater— the realm of the birds refers to Alcibiades' foolhardy Sicilian Expedition which led to Athens' fall. These comedies are interventions in reality; the characters they present and play with are not abstract but, rather, the most concrete of all —the statesmen, philosophers, poets and generals of the day: Kolon,[1] Demosthenes, Euripides, who Aristophanes couldn't help getting worked up about, devising ever-new outrageous situations to ridicule him. And finally Socrates must be seen as Aristophanes' victim—the dangerous ridicule of his comedy *The Clouds* had a deadly effect.

Let me further voice the suspicion that the antagonism between Old Attic Comedy (Aristophanes) and New Attic Comedy (Menander) was more than a family feud. To the extent documented, New Attic Comedy no longer possessed the central, forceful stroke of creativity—the power to transform the world into a comedy. It was not the comedy of society but comedy in society, not political but apolitical. It no longer centred on specific personalities from everyday life but on specific types—the procuress, the foolish peasant, the widow, the miser, the bragging soldier. Its technique had moved towards that of tragedy.

Like all that is not dependent on creativity, New Attic Comedy created a trend. Its material was passed on from poet to poet. What was important was no longer the stroke

---

1 Possibly a typo for Cleon (d. 422 BCE), a demagogue criticized by Aristophanes, or Solon (638–538 BCE), a statesman mentioned in several of his plays.

of creativity but the creative conceits, the punch lines, often no more than the artful execution, the potential for variation and, more and more crucially, the psychology. Its path led via Menander and Plautus to Molière, in whom it reached its zenith. He is not the wittiest poet but the most precise, the most perfect in his mastery of his tools. Fittingly, even today the French perform him entirely from the outside, without losing his demonic character—not from the inside, as we are forced to do in German, lacking his language, his precision. In this way New Attic Comedy established a dynasty that exists to this day; the French theatre's romantic triangle comedies descend from it, and Christopher Fry's superb *A Phoenix Too Frequent* (1946) is one of its latest triumphs. That even Aristophanes leads up to them proves how necessary was their advent, how legitimate their triumphant advance.

The path taken by Old Attic Comedy is harder to trace, more a case for the criminologists of literary history than for me. And only fragments have come down to us from the other poets who, with Aristophanes, made up Old Attic Comedy. By its very nature it is too grotesque and idiosyncratic to have made its way unscathed into a different age. Too political not to be dependent on politics and too crude to take its place in the realm of aesthetics, it vanished from the stage at its zenith. I admit that Carlo Gozzi's art, Ferdinand Raimund's fairy-tale farces, Johann Nestroy's theatre takes after it (though equally so after New Attic Comedy), but I see no particular sense in giving in to the obvious temptation to divide the world of comedy into an Old Attic and a New Attic continent—key regions would lie scattered between them as islands, embroiled in a senseless war. I see Shakespeare's comedies *Measure for Measure* and *The Tempest* above all as prodigious new creations in this genre, like Heinrich von Kleist's *Amphytrion* (1807) and *The Broken Jug*

(1808)—these are allegories of the human situation, comedies that express the ultimate intellectual freedom precisely because they are not tragedies. But Aristophanes does have his heirs, no doubt about it. Among the Germans Frank Wedekind,[2] Bertolt Brecht and Karl Kraus; among the French, in many ways, Jean Giraudoux. But Aristophanic art regains its purest expression in a different literary genre: Rabelais' *Gargantua* describes the life of a giant in contemporary France; in Swift, Gulliver first meets dwarfs, then giants, finally marooned on an island of intelligent horses and animal-like humans; Don Quixote, the Knight of Sad Countenance, believes in the giants and fairies of his books; and Nikolai Gogol's Chichikov buys up dead peasants. All these stories bear a striking similarity to a plot by Aristophanes. As with him, a stroke of creativity alters reality, elevating it to the grotesque. As with the Greek, creativity is the explosion that forms this cosmos.

But what gives Aristophanes current relevance is the question of distance. The tragedies present a past as though it were present, overcoming distance in order to shake us to the core. Aristophanes, that great master of comedy—why shouldn't we deduce dramatic principles from him for once, from his position, as we've long done with the tragic poets?—takes the opposite approach. By setting his comedies in the present, he creates distance, and that, I believe, is crucial for a comedy. From this it follows that a topical play can only be a comedy in the spirit of Aristophanes, for the sake of the distance which, after all, it is able to create, for I can think of no other point for a topical play than this.

It is important to appreciate that there are two kinds of grotesqueness: grotesqueness for the sake of a romanticism

---

2 Frank Wedekind (1864–1918): Socially critical German playwright.

that aims to evoke fear or outlandish emotions (e.g. by having a ghost appear) and grotesqueness for the sake of the distance which can be created only by this means. It is no coincidence that the grotesque allowed Aristophanes, Rabelais and Swift to set their plots *in* their time, write plays of their time, mean *their* time. The grotesque is an extreme stylization, a sudden visualization, and it is precisely for this reason that it can address issues of the time, and still more, the present itself, without becoming tendentious or journalistic. For this reason I can well imagine a gruesome grotesque of the Second World War but not a tragedy, not yet, as we can't yet have the proper distance. Thus not only Don Quixote and Sancho Panza but also Aristophanes' *Birds*. This art does not, like tragedy, seek to share in suffering—it seeks to depict. And so Gulliver's grotesque travels are like a retort in which four different experiments demonstrate human weaknesses and limitations. The grotesque is one of the greatest possibilities of being precise. It cannot be denied that this art has the cruelty of objectivity, but it is the art of the moralist, not the nihilist, of salt, not rot. It is a matter of wit and keen intelligence (which is why the Enlightenment was expert at it) rather than the now-sentimental, now-frivolous smugness the audience takes for humour. It is uncomfortable, but necessary . . .

AMERICAN AND EUROPEAN DRAMA

1959

Ladies and Gentlemen,

In Europe, one often hears that the main difference between American and European theatre consists in the fact that America's great dramatists write realistically, even naturalistically, in contrast to the Europeans who are abstract, more speculative, who in short constitute the avant-garde. Admittedly this is a very sweeping judgement, but it is a judgement one often hears. In Europe, American theatre is denounced as conservative, accused of ultimately doing no more than European theatre did before it in the time of Henrik Ibsen, Gerhart Hauptmann and Anton Chekhov; meanwhile, European theatre is accused of getting bogged down in experiments, losing touch with reality and, what is worse, with the audience.

It can't be denied that this view has a certain basis in truth. There is no doubt that future literary scholars will gain a much more vivid picture of contemporary America from contemporary American plays than of Europe from European plays; on the other hand, European plays will clearly offer more information about our contemporary philosophy, or rather non-philosophy, our doubts and our difficulties. But to postulate the superiority of European over American literature on this basis is not only wrong but dilettantish. The contrast which begins to emerge here is of quite a different nature. Just as today only two great powers remain—unfortunately, and not at all to the world's benefit —today, now that one of these great powers has ceased to play an important role in contemporary literature, there is only one great power that produces literature, significant literature, namely American literature, as against the literature of small states.

My hunch about this may surprise you. My hunch is that the difference between American and European drama consists in the fact that a dramatist who belongs to a great power will behave very differently, aspire to a very different theatre, a very different theatrical style than a dramatist from a small state. If true, this distinction is much more important than one might at first believe. American theatre as a result of America's great power assumes an almost tragic position at the moment when we understand it as an attempt to see itself, to keep from losing itself. Every giant power by nature grows to become uncanny, inhuman, abstract, whether or not it wants to, independent of its aspirations, of its will; instils fear, outwardly, through its sheer presence, posing a threat without meaning to through the sheer possibility of rape inherent in it; isolates itself, grows lonely; but inwardly too, along with the feelings of power and freedom it instils in its citizens, it inspires the sense of being faced with something uncontrollable, impersonal, arbitrary, fateful, faceless, indeed blind in its fury. In this vast technical environment, writers, especially dramatists, assume a very specific role which they perform, are forced to perform, instinctively or consciously. Drama is bound to the portrayal of people; each drama erects a world of bodies; the building blocks of drama are and always will be people. To dramatize is to humanize, and contemporary American dramatists humanize the great continental power they live in, give back the present its face, wresting it from abstraction by shattering, in a sense, the vast environment, condensing it into a milieu. The art form of today's great states is realism. But this is not escapism, not a turn to provincialism. It is not the case, for example, that because his plays are set mainly in the American South, Tennessee Williams can be understood only by southerners; on the contrary, this is exactly what makes him international. He is barred from the very possibility of provincialism because the world's interest in America is too keen. We breathe a sigh of relief—the Americans are people like us, the same flaws, the same vices, the same goodness! We find a countenance, a face; a spectre takes on familiar contours, an idol is humanized. And I'd like to note, albeit in passing, that the same goes for pre-communist Russian literature; the Russian novel and the Russian theatre have a great deal in common with American literature. But don't get me wrong: Eugene O'Neill, Tennessee Williams, Arthur Miller are great dramatists not because they are American citizens—they would still be so if they were, say, Liechtensteiners, but then they would write differently.

And so this brings us to the question: How does the writer of a small state write? How, to choose a very small state, does the Liechtensteiner write? Now, I don't know if there are any Liechtensteiners who write dramas, but I can picture a Liechtensteiner writing a play set in the milieu of a Vaduz bus driver. The play is performed at a Swiss-Liechtensteinian Friendship Week in Sankt Gallen and gets a warm reception; at the launch party the director even assures the author over coffee with kirsch that he finds the play far more poetic than Williams' *Cat on a Hot Tin Roof* (1955), but that is the end of that. The author is very sad and curses the fate that made him a Liechtensteiner. But I can picture a completely different writer, a writer who derives immense pleasure from being a Liechtensteiner and nothing but, a writer for whom Liechtenstein is much more, infinitely more than the sixty-one square miles which it actually measures. For this writer, Liechtenstein becomes a model of the world, he condenses it by expanding it, making Vaduz into a Babylon and its prince, say, a Nebuchadnezzar. The Liechtensteiners protest, finding everything wildly exaggerated, missing the Liechtensteinian yodel and the Liechtensteinian cheese industry, but this writer isn't just played in Sankt Gallen, he goes international, because his invented Liechtenstein mirrors the world. This Liechtensteinian writer has to keep trying out new ideas, making Liechtenstein into an ever-new model of the world. As a dramatist, he is forced to blaze revolutionary paths, and these new paths are the right ones because he has no other paths left.

This Liechtensteinian dramatist I have invented here can be found again and again in all small states. Think of Strindberg or Ibsen or Beckett today or Frisch, my Swiss colleague, or if you like, think a little about me, or about the role of the Irish in Anglo-Saxon literature. But also of Kleist and Büchner, back in the days of the small German states, while typically enough Hauptmann belongs to the only epoch in which Germany, sadly, was a great state, and Brecht once again, crucially, belongs to the small state of Germany[1]—you see that I have no political illusions as a European. Now, of course it makes a difference whether a state is already aware that it's a small state or whether it still believes in its greatness without really being great—this might explain Brecht's communist leanings—but I believe I can pronounce the law that once a state has decisively installed itself as a small state, it provides writers with a completely new freedom. Namely, the freedom to take the state as what it is meant to be—a technical necessity, not a man-eating myth. The installed, technologically and

[1] That is, the GDR, where Brecht spent his final years.

civilizationally tamed small state such as we find in Europe has defused itself politically; now its problem is the world as a whole and that makes the world its writers' problem. One of the major proofs of this thesis is Ibsen. As a writer from a small state, he forged the weapons for writers from the great states because not only his society but society at large became a problem for him. The writer from a small nation, in my somewhat malicious definition, can't afford to be too patriotic if only because it would hurt business. But I am not trying to define values, ladies and gentlemen, to assign marks. Good writing is always equal in value. And above all, if I draw a distinction here between dramatists from great powers and those from small states, I am identifying only a very general, almost static law. There are always exceptions—think of Gotthelf, think of Wilder—for, ultimately, writing has its roots in human freedom; it is one of the few proofs that it exists.

GEORG BÜCHNER AND THE PRINCIPLE OF CAUSE

1986

All that Georg Büchner undertook, he did out of passion, while pretending it was to earn money, which he had to earn indeed, as in 1835 he began making preparations to emigrate to Switzerland. In exile, in Strasbourg, in 1836, he wrote to Karl Gutzkow[1]—who had served one month of a three-month term in a Mannheim prison for disparaging the beliefs of the Christian community—that he too was in prison, in the dullest one under the sun, day and night he'd written a treatise, long, broad and deep, on this odious subject, he didn't know where he'd found the patience, but he was obsessed with the idea of giving a lecture course on the development of German philosophy since Cartesius next semester in Zurich; for that he needed a diploma, and people didn't seem inclined to bestow a doctorate upon his dear son Danton.[2] What else could he possibly have done? But the treatise to which Büchner alludes in his letter to Gutzkow—the one on Cartesius, as René Descartes Latinized his name, and Baruch Spinoza, both of whom attempted a strictly rational practice of metaphysics according to a mathematical method —is important not only in terms of describing the German philosophy that followed them; it would have been equally necessary to explore English philosophy as preparation. One

Acceptance speech for the 1986 Georg Büchner Prize awarded by the German Academy for Language and Literature.

1 Karl Gutzkow (1811–78): German writer, Büchner's first sponsor.

2 Büchner's play *Danton's Death* (1835).

cannot entirely dismiss the suspicion that he was attempting to use these two last—apart from Leibnitz'—radical metaphysics to examine how far it is possible to get with mathematics. On Cartesius he had noted that it is God who fills the abyss between thought and understanding, between subject and object; He is the bridge between the *cogito, ergo sum*, between lonely, erring thought, certain of one thing alone, self-consciousness, and the outside world. The experiment turns out rather naively, he finds, but one sees with what instinctive precision Cartesius had already measured philosophy's grave; it's strange, to be sure, how he uses the Good Lord as a ladder to climb out. And on Spinoza he noted that Spinozism is the enthusiasm of mathematics; in it, the Cartesian method of demonstration finds its consummation and closure, only here does it achieve its full implications. Kant had shattered the metaphysics of both. His *Critique of Pure Reason* had appeared in 1781, closer in time to Büchner than Heidegger's *Being and Time* (1927) to us. The ramifications of a philosophy and the possibility of developing it further are more important than its validity. Kant sundered science from philosophy. He proceeded from a paradox. He tried to prove Newton's physics philosophically, to ask why a mathematical science is possible at all. He declared mathematics to be useful solely for experience, for which metaphysics was useless. He divided the world into a physical one that can be experienced through the forms of our representations and the categories of our thought and a realm that by nature lies beyond all possible experience, that of the thing in itself, while questions regarding God, the soul, freedom, immortality remained unprovable. As he wrote, he could not even assume God, freedom, immortality with a view to the necessary practical use of reason without simultaneously depriving speculative reason of its pretensions towards exalted insights. By denying philosophy the right to continue pursuing it, Kant caused metaphysics to lose its importance, all the more so as Kant placed pure reason under the primacy of practical reason. 'Should' was more important to him than 'must'; what cannot be proved by pure reason had to be postulated by practical reason, all the sublimities, the soul, God, freedom; but what can only be postulated need not be postulated, the radical evil in man forces him, when he tries to subject himself to practical reason, to act against his inclinations, one of Kant's insights that outraged Goethe. The *Critique of Practical Reason* (1788) is not only a philosophy of the duty, dictated by reason, to which a responsible person must submit, but above all a philosophy of 'as if', a philosophy of fiction, replacing metaphysics with a system of moral postulates. On its publication in 1788 it delighted Schiller, who saw it as the philosophy of freedom, while it outraged those who pretended to believe but wanted people to believe that they believed, while those who believed needed no proof of their belief, believing anyway that through their belief they knew the truth, and the philosophers meanwhile took pains to avoid the issues Kant had raised because they were unable to resolve them—the result was the systems of German idealism. In 1807, three years after Kant's death, Hegel wrote *The Phenomenology of Spirit*, 1812 saw the publication of his *Logic*, in 1814 Fichte[3] died, in 1818 Schopenhauer's *The World as Will and Representation* appeared. Hegel died in 1831. Schelling[4] and Hölderlin[5] survived Büchner as ghosts. Feuerbach,[6] born nine years

3 Johann Gottlieb Fichte (1762–1814): One of the founding figures of German idealism.

4 Friedrich Wilhelm Joseph Schelling (1775–1854): German idealist philospher.

5 Friedrich Hölderlin (1770–1843): German romantic-idealist poet, friend of Hegel and Schelling.

6 Ludwig von Feuerbach (1804–72): German philosopher, influenced dialectical materialism.

before Büchner, and Marx, born three years after him, wrote their major works only after Büchner's death. But Büchner never did describe the philosophical epoch which had preceded him and in which he lived. The doctorate which he craved for his *Danton* was bestowed on him by the University of Zurich for the lecture 'On the Nervous System of the Barbel'—a common fish in Strasbourg—which he had delivered there before the Society of Sciences in April and May 1836. Büchner was catapulted from philosophy to science. On 12 October 1836, he immigrated to Zurich and by early November had already delivered at the university his trial lecture, 'On Cranial Nerves', in which he identified two fundamental views in the physiological and anatomical sciences. According to him, the first, predominant in England and France, regarded all phenomena of organic life from a teleological perspective, finding the riddle's solution in the purpose. It made the skull into an artificial buttressed vault designed to protect its occupant, the brain; the cheeks and lips into a masticatory and respiratory apparatus; the eye into a complex lens; the lids and lashes into its curtains; even the tears were merely the droplets that kept it moist. The teleological method moved in perpetual circles, he argued, for one must inquire after the purpose of this purpose, leading inevitably to a *progressus in infinitum*; but nature did not act according to purposes, in all its expressions it was immediately sufficient unto itself. All that existed, existed for its own sake. To seek the law of this existence was the goal of the philosophical approach, dominant in Germany, which countered the teleological one. All that was purpose in the one philosophy became effect in the other, and so for this philosophical method the entire physical existence of the individual was not summoned up for its own preservation; rather, this existence became the manifestation of a primal law, a law of beauty which brought forth the highest and purest forms from the simplest lines and sketches. The inquiry into such a law automatically led to the two springs of understanding which had fuelled the enthusiasm of absolute knowledge since times immemorial—the intuition of the mystic, and the dogmatism of the rational philosopher. Critics would be forced to admit that it had so far proved impossible to bridge the gap between the latter and the natural life that was perceived directly. Philosophy a priori was still stuck in a desolate waste, a long distance from fresh green life, and it was highly questionable whether it would ever cover this distance. In its ingenious attempts to make headway it had been forced to make do with the resigned notion that its endeavours were not about achieving a goal but about the endeavour itself. I would like to mention two more passages. In one he explained that one could trace the steps leading from the simplest organism whose nervous activity consisted solely in a dull coenaesthesia to the gradual articulation and development of particular sensory organs. Their senses were nothing new that had been added, they merely raised the existing to a higher power. Somewhat later he noted that it would probably always prove futile to tackle the problem by examining the most intricate form, that of the human being. The simplest forms were always the safest guides, manifesting only the primal, the absolutely essential. What is striking about this lecture—a scientific one, after all—is that the twenty-three-year-old Büchner describes the fundamental view that guides him as a philosophical one. As he had previously entertained the idea of lecturing on recent German philosophy in Zurich, it is not that far-fetched to assume that this lecture on cranial nerves contains a philosophy of his own. It is all the more surprising that he describes as 'German' the method which he sets against the teleological one and which consists of seeking in the law of beauty the reason why nature in all its expressions is itself. In so doing he goes against both Kant and his successors—in Kant the method and in his successors the philosophy. According to Kant, a scientific theory can express only a causal necessity; but purpose is not a category of pure reason and thus not a constitutive principle of objective knowledge, though in the case of what cannot be explained by pure reason, such as life, since the essence of the living organism consists in the fact that the whole is determined by the parts just as the parts are determined by the whole, the impression of purposefulness inevitably emerges. As a hypothetical principle, the teleological method is a given with regard to the living organism, as a method which supposes that this organism has a purpose in order to trace the causal natural relationships. By contrast, post-Kantian philosophy was inherently teleological. To ask about the purpose is to ask about the meaning, which Kant also made into a matter of practical reason, into something subjective—by setting a purpose for itself, the will also sets its meaning, eternal peace is the wish that this peace should not, as Kant puts it, take place 'only on the vast graveyard of the human race'.[7] The idealism that followed Kant again ascribed to what it postulated behind the world of phenomena, be it the I or the Absolute or the World Spirit, an objective meaning, a purpose towards which it develops, an obvious impossibility given the unpredictability of human nature and social systems, culminating in Marx in the steamroller of natural law leading to the classless and stateless society, to the freedom of humankind. Büchner would have asked the purpose of this purpose,   the meaning of this meaning, whether it in turn would not lead meaninglessly

7 Immanuel Kant, 'Perpetual Peace' in *Kant: Political Writings* (Hans Reiss ed., H. B. Nisbet trans.) (Cambridge: Cambridge University Press, 1991), pp. 93–130; here, p. 96.

to new classes, to a new state, to a new unfreedom and so forth. Büchner was a rebel, Marx a revolutionary. Büchner was outraged by the status quo, Marx saw it as a confirmation of his thinking. Büchner saw how people thwart themselves, Marx overlooked people. Büchner was a realist, seeing the relationship between poor and rich as the only revolutionary element in the world. Behind Marx looms Hegel, his dialectics adopted from Fichte, thesis, antithesis, synthesis, the World Spirit's blood-churning strides through time. But Büchner, as a scientist, is indebted to Goethe, whose importance for comparative anatomy lies not only in his discovery of the human intermaxillary bone but still more in his views on this science; the notion that a living being is brought forth for certain purposes and that its form is determined accordingly by an intentional primal force as he wrote around 1790 in his *Towards a General Comparative Theory*. This faculty of teleological imagination was in itself pious, agreeable to certain dispositions, essential to certain notions, but was trivial, like all trivial things, because on the whole it was convenient and adequate to human nature, for man was accustomed to valuing things only insofar as they were useful to him and, since by nature and circumstances he had to regard himself as the ultimate product of creation, why shouldn't he also believe that he was its ultimate and final purpose? Why shouldn't his vanity permit itself the minor sophism? Because he needed things and was able to use them, he concluded that they were created in order to be used by him. He would sooner attribute the genesis of the thistle which made work on his field a torment to the curse of a wrathful good being, the spite of a mischievous evil being, than see this thistle as a child of great, universal nature, just as dear to her heart as the painstakingly cultivated, so highly esteemed wheat. But would he not respect nature's primal force still more if he assumed that its force is contingent and learnt to see that it could just as easily shape from the outside as towards the outside, from the inside as towards the inside? *The fish exists for the water* seemed to say much less than *the fish exists in water and through water*, for the latter expressed much more clearly what in the first was hidden and obscure—that the existence of a creature which we call a fish is possible only under the condition of an element which we call water, not only in order to be in it but also to become in it. What Büchner calls the law of beauty is for Goethe the ideal design of the animal form, the morphology of the animal form which also includes the human form. This transformation of form whose purpose lies in itself, not outside itself, is still regarded metaphysically, philosophically, because it presupposes a primal form of the animal, a primal image, which is why Büchner accuses teleological thinking of a *progressus in infinitum* while disregarding the fact that if he describes as an effect what goal-directed thinking calls a purpose, then this effect must have a cause, and even if this cause is the law of beauty, then this law must feature a cause as its effect. The principle of the cause, that nothing is without a cause, leads to a *regressus in infinitum*, knowing no prime cause, to assume which, according to Kant, would be an antinomy, putting reason in conflict with itself; pre-Kantian philosophy assumed it, God being the prime cause, the *causa sui*, the cause of itself, while post-Kantian science no longer had to concern itself with the prime cause, for philosophy was not its affair; some, like Büchner, still hesitated, having not yet come up against the implacable law of evolution, and then, of necessity. There being no other choice, science plunged into the maelstrom of causes, into the greatest, boldest and most perilous adventure which the human mind has ever undertaken, for by confronting nature it confronts itself; it was she who enlightened Man. While Marx declared that philosophy's task is to change the world, not to interpret it, it was now science that changed the world, more than politics or war ever could, and it did so by interpreting the world in such a way that it always checked its interpretations against reality in order to arrive at ever-new interpretations, proceeding as it were from error to error, advancing from one putative cause to further putative causes, climbing up and down to ever-new theories and hypotheses, finally even bursting the boundaries which Kant had assigned it and conquering realms which he had regarded as inconceivable, for he underestimated the human imagination, which is capable of breaking even the barrier of the sensory and the concrete, now venturing questions once posed only by metaphysicians. Since Kant, there have been two cultures—scientific and literary. The scientific culture leads to a lack of knowledge, for this lack increases the more one knows, while the literary culture, to the extent it still considers itself philosophy, runs about helpless as a rat in the labyrinth of language and lets itself be used, like the religions, to back up those in power or striving for power; insofar as it is literature, it has become utterly ineffectual, unless one ascribes significance to fashion. Culture is the outfit of the moment, either off the rack or custom-made. Literature's total superfluity is its only justification. There is none more sublime. We are living in a Socratic world. In many ways, literary culture can be compared with sophism, which turns circles within its own terminology, and the exact sciences with Plato's attempt to penetrate the world of ideas—as we attempt to grasp reality using the objective methods of mathematics, which has its subjective roots in the nature of our mind, this reality turns out again and again to be a mere idea, albeit couched in the beauty of a formula. Socrates would have been indifferent to this problem; he, who preferred listening to himself, because he could daydream or doze at the same time, would have laughed at our philosophy and yawned at our literature. Knowing that he knew nothing, like Kant he would have known only one good thing in the world—the good will. He would have been interested only in practical reason; in astonishment, he would have watched it conquer the realm of pure reason, bringing such necessary, useful, useless and deadly spoils; he would have frowned to find humanity building not a safer world but one increasingly prone to catastrophe, in which peace is gradually becoming just as dangerous as war and war is no longer war but an atomic Auschwitz of the human race that will vaporize not only its bodies but its spirit, and more than that—all the grandiose things it ever brought forth, Homer, the Greek tragedies, Lear's ravings, Bach's Art of the Fugue, Beethoven's quartets and the Christ of the Isenheim Altar, sweeping up from his tomb, nothing left but the Pyramids, standing there senselessly, mausoleums of the pharaohs and humanity alike, of the mighty and their victims—and already holding the cup of hemlock he would have shaken his head to see humanity proved unequal to the knowledge that it knows nothing and, more superstitious than ever, foundering upon enlightenment, and to see that wherever they are free they abuse freedom so greatly that it might soon make no difference whether they are free or unfree, and not without irony he would conclude, draining the cup of hemlock, that despite so many reasons to grow wiser, we have fallen prey not to practical reason but to practical unreason. And so we look back, just a hundred and fifty years ago, when the wheels of the scientific and technical age were slowly set in motion. We see the eerie image of Georg Büchner, émigré, drafter of a political pamphlet against the Hessian government, known to a few as the author of a wild play about the French Revolution but still undiscovered as a dramatic revolutionary, in November

1836, four years after Goethe's death and three months before his own end, convinced of history's ghastly fatalism, of the appalling sameness of human nature and the inescapable violence of the human condition, we see him begin work as a private lecturer for about twenty students in Zurich, by day wielding the scalpel in passionately defiant search of the law of beauty, dissecting fish, frogs and toads and preparing them for his lectures, holding the magnifier to his short-sighted eyes, by night sitting over his books at Spiegelgasse 12, writing *Woyzeck*:

> DOCTOR. Gentlemen, here I am on the roof like David when he spied Bathsheba; but all I see are knickers on the line in the girls' boarding school garden. Gentlemen, we come now to the important question of the relationship between subject and object. If we examine one of those creatures in which the divine spark achieves a high degree of organic expression, and if we investigate its relationship to space, the earth and the planetary universe—if, gentlemen, I throw this cat out of the window, what will be the instinctive behavior of such a creature relative to its centre of gravity?— Woyzeck. (*He roars.*) Woyzeck!
>
> WOYZECK (*catches the cat*). Doctor, it bites!
>
> DOCTOR. You fool, you're as gentle as if it were your own grandmother.
>
> WOYZECK. Doctor, I'm all of a tremble.
>
> DOCTOR (*delighted*). Are you indeed! (*Rubs his hands, takes the cat.*) What's this, gentlemen? A new species of animal louse. And a very fine one.
>
> (*Produces a magnifying glass. The cat runs away.*)
>
> Animals have no scientific instincts. I'll show you something else instead. Observe. For three months

this man has eaten nothing but peas. Note the effect, feel for yourselves. What an irregular pulse—and the eyes!

WOYZECK. Doctor, everything's gone dark.[8]

---

8 Georg Büchner, *Danton's Death, Leonce and Lena, Woyzeck* (Victor Price trans.) (New York: Oxford University Press, 2008), p. 124.

ART AND SCIENCE;

OR, PLATO;

OR, CREATIVITY, VISION AND IDEA;

OR, A DIFFICULT FORM OF ADDRESS;

OR, BEGINNING AND END OF A PUBLIC ADDRESS

1984

Fifteen years ago, I held a public address as part of the *studium generale* at the Johannes Gutenberg University in Mainz, and it puzzles me in retrospect how ingenuously I began with 'ladies and gentlemen'. Certainly, it's a polite form of address, nothing wrong with politeness, but sometimes it is puzzling and should have puzzled me even then, and not only after cable television made me realize the exquisite ceremoniousness of this form of address, standing as it did in contrast to the way the addressees proceeded to behave. I am all the more surprised today that the students were so friendly towards me. What female student, indeed, who at all likes to be addressed as a 'lady' and what gentleman doesn't bridle when addressed as a 'gentleman'? He'd put up with it at most from a hairdresser or a waiter. But the 'my' is suspect as well. With a waiter or hairdresser one acquiesces, it belongs to his professional jargon, and if a surgeon says to me, 'My dear, esteemed fellow, won't you lie down, let's tackle your liver, the stomach must go, it's not vital, and let's see what else you can spare, as long as you're open,' the 'my' is perfectly appropriate and for better or worse I must accept the 'dear, esteemed fellow' as well, containing as it does all the affection towards my innards, comparable only with the affection and esteem with which a gourmet regards his steak. But 'my dear listeners' or 'my esteemed audience'? Let's not even discuss the 'dear' and 'esteemed'; the dubiousness would know no bounds, already knows no bounds; and the 'mine' too is still suspect—you aren't at my mercy, the doors aren't locked, no one stops you from fleeing or falling asleep, though this does inhibit me from addressing you as 'listeners', you've come of your own accord, not under compulsion, you're not mine, you're yourselves. While 'listeners' is eliminated by those who fall asleep during my address, 'audience' confronts me with new difficulties—audience means the entirety of all who are gathered here; the salutation 'O audience' is comical but logically correct, nothing stands in its way as a form of address, but everything stands in the way of the address which this form of address is supposed to introduce, so severely does the form of address obstruct the address that, strictly speaking, it becomes impossible to hold it at all, 'audience' being a general term which it is impossible to speak to or even of. If I attempt to concretize this general term to mean you who are gathered here, it can be no more than an attempt, for who are you, you who are listening to me? Certainly I hope that everyone can hear me, that the auditorium's acoustics are good, but I don't just want to be heard—I want to be understood; and it's not everyone who decides whether I'm understood but each individual one of everyone, each individual one of you; then again, this individual who understands or these individuals who understand don't make up the audience, just a part of it whose size I don't know, whereby nothing in the world can prove whether the various individuals who understand me understand me immediately or in fact misunderstand me immediately. And so when I talk I must talk to something phantom-like, to something simultaneously concrete and fictitious, to all yet not to all, to each yet not to each. If I talk nonetheless, it is only because I talk myself into the notion that I am talking to an ideal audience, an audience consisting entirely of individuals who understand me perfectly. This ideal audience exists only as an idea, I can think of this audience, not imagine it, it is the rhetorical guideline along which I try to reach each individual. I make an effort to talk so understandably that everyone seems to me to understand me but, as I will never know whether I have achieved this goal once I've talked, I have no choice but to talk as though each individual were all individuals; in a strict sense, I am talking not to listeners but to a fictitious listener and this fictitious listener who stands for all listeners is I for I alone can know whether I understand myself—thus I have become my own audience and you have dissolved into thin air. But of course my failure to address you is merely prophylactic, to draw your attention to certain complications that will emerge in my address, not merely in the form of my address. Just as the difficulty in the form of address reflects on the one hand the speaker's difficulty in imagining his audience and on the other hand the audience's difficulty in achieving clarity about itself, which in turn points to a central difficulty of our age, its inability to come to terms with itself, under such auspices the topic of my address also harbours difficulties and pitfalls which should surprise neither me who must hold it nor you who must hold out until it's over. An address on the relationship of art to science and science to art is just as difficult or just as easy as an address on the relationship of a person to the Good Lord, or the other way round, assuming one knows what the Good Lord is supposed to be—I don't know myself. And so the difficulty of my chosen form of address is hardly worth mentioning compared with the difficulty of my address. This has nothing to do with the difficulty in which questions such as 'Is Beuys still art?' or 'Is astrology science?' land us. It has to do with the difficulty experienced by every writer when asked 'Why do you write, anyway?' or 'Why does science claim something is true and then suddenly proclaim the opposite?' Naive questions which one prefers to avoid, for it is natural that a scientist can err, the possibility of error is just as much a part of science as the possibility of finding things out. Hamlet was not written in order to declare 'to be or not to be', he holds this monologue only to play the madman, a cruel ruse with which he tricks the court and drives Ophelia insane, and Albert Einstein did not set down his famous formula in order to enable the atom bomb. Behind all this lies more than the purely personal, behind all this lies the history of the human mind.

First, strokes of creativity, for example, to thrust a dry stick into the flames of a tree kindled by lightning and carry off the burning branch to kindle other dry branches, overcoming the primitive human fear of fire which we shared with animals, and making humans human; later, visions; finally, ideas. All words for the same thing, one might think. But words are like a painter's tools—some things can best be captured with a brush, some with a piece of charcoal and some with a pen. The solar system is composed not only of planets and their moons but also of a plethora of planetoids (minor and dwarf planets), rocks and debris, clouds of dust and gas, chunks, pellets and crystals of ice. Like the earth, man also finds himself in a solar system, that of the human mind. He is surrounded not only by the primal motives, memories, fears and desires of humanity, representing the planets, but also by the residual experience of long-vanished peoples, by myths, sagas, fairy tales, whole showers of tomes, folios, trashy novels, classics, paperbacks, by Saturn's rings and news reports, films, TV series, etc., etc. Just as, to

use a different image, man lives not only in an atmosphere
but also in a biosphere, in a soup of micro-organisms, bac-
teria, bacilli, viruses, etc., he also lives in a 'noosphere', in
the totality of all human thought, quibbling, belief, opinion,
dreaming, fear, superstition, metaphysicizing and fantasiz-
ing, while at the same time each person also lives in his own
sphere of experience, in all that constitutes his successes and
failures, his loving and being loved, his disappointments and
humiliations. Strokes of creativity point to this human and
individual state of affairs—these fragments of thought are
suddenly there, no one can name their inventor, like mete-
ors they've shot into the visible part of the noosphere and
flared up, into the atmosphere which is also part of the solar
system, but they come from its invisible part—after all, we
don't see a comet until it has come so close to the sun that
its ice begins to vaporize; the part of the solar system 'invisible' to us is incomparably larger than the 'visible' part, a
planet beyond Pluto remains to be discovered and comets
can travel light years away from the sun before returning.
And so each stroke of creativity in the history of the mind
can be traced back only as far as we can survey this history
(and we know less about it than we imagine), even if the
one who had it is oblivious; someone else was struck before
him and someone else before him. If its origins are uncertain, its future is no less so. It is important not only that it
strikes but, still more, whom it strikes and why. The vision
has a broader spectrum than the idea or the creative notion.
In the idea lies thought, in creativity lies violence, one
almost has to apologize for being struck by creativity; the
vision points to something sensual, it is primordial, which
it has in common with creativity, while the idea has something derivative, intellectual. If we relegate creativity to
technology, visions to art and ideas to science, this is but a
working hypothesis, no more. Neither technology nor art

nor science can do without creativity, visions and ideas. The working hypothesis is meaningful nonetheless. Having compared the noosphere of man, whose psychic composition emerged in his prehistory, with the solar system and the creativity with the meteor, we can compare the vision with a mighty solar eruption that illuminates the solar system as a whole, once the Ptolemaic vision, later the Copernican, while the idea represents the gravitational force that formed the solar system. But visions and ideas strike as well. A commentary on Aristotle states that Leucippus of Miletus[1] thought up atoms 'since he observed that coming to be and change are unceasing in things that are';[2] this opinion is not false, but even primitive humans made the observations which the commentary ascribes to Leucippus. Primitive humans found permanence, the non-changing, in animate nature, later still in the gods, visions that secured their survival. As in the Ice Age the glaciers carried boulders along with them, depositing them when the ice receded, evolution carries experiences which human beings encapsulate in ever-new visions. It may have taken hundreds of millennia and longer still, long past the Stone Age, until they marvelled anew at what they'd known for ages—that everything disintegrates, decomposes, decays or, ground down by time, turns to sand. Some, like primitive humans, searched for permanence, denying change; Leucippus affirmed it. I'd like to call these first philosophers visionaries, but their visions too are carried along by the mind's evolution. Xenophanes of Colophon in Asia Minor lived between 565 and 470 BCE

1 Leucippus of Miletus (5th century BCE): Greek philosopher regarded by some as the founder of atomism and the teacher of Democritus who developed a more extensive atomic theory.

2 Cited in Richard D. McKirahan, *Philosophy Before Socrates: An Introduction with Texts and Commentary* (Indianapolis: Hackett, 1994), p. 306.

and, expelled by the Persians, settled in Elea in Lower Italy and was active as a rhapsodist, reciting Homer and Hesiod. Tiring of his profession, he announced that the poets whose works he chanted had imputed to the gods all that was infamy and ignominy for human beings—robbery, adultery and mutual deception. If cows, horses or lions had hands and could paint, the horses would depict gods like horses and the cows would depict them like cows, creating forms such as they themselves had. In reality, he claimed, there is only one god, spherical as the universe and in no way resembling man. 'As a whole he sees, as a whole he thinks and as a whole he hears.'[3] Xenophanes chiselled this vision, more powerful than the Jews' One God, from a boulder which was carried to him from primaeval times, already worked by Homer and Hesiod. Xenophanes' critique of Homer has been forgotten, but the perfection he attributed to the sphere, whose surface points are all equidistant from its centre, lives on not only in Parmenides, whose 'being' is a perfect orb, but also in Plato's spherical cosmos and Aristotle's dogma of the spherical motion of the heavenly bodies, from which not even Galileo was able to free himself, on to the modern conception of the cosmos which compares it to an expanding bubble formed by an exploding sphere of material, with the points on the bubble, the galaxies, moving apart at an ever-growing speed. We have but a few fragments of Xenophanes, his writings have been lost, but a thing once thought and written, and be it by others, is never lost entirely, it may be forgotten but it re-emerges, is transformed, embellished with new facts, hypotheses and theories, even if the one who first thought it has long since been forgotten. Of Leucippus, too, we know little. When he

3 Cited in M. R. Wright, *Introducing Greek Philosophy* (Berkeley: University of California Press, 2010), p. 87.

speaks, as Aristotle relates, of the full and the empty, of being and non-being, this vision, as extravagant and absurd as all first visions, fantastic forays of the human mind into the barely thinkable, was preceded by a long incubation period—it was embedded in the experience of things until the realization that there is no consistency of things in experience led to the vision of the extra-experiential atoms, to the ultimate particle conceived as consistent; and as each particle presupposes space in order to be a particle at all, the concept of empty space was inevitable—the atoms and empty space are one and the same vision. We do not know how it came about. Perhaps Leucippus lay on a beach somewhere, above him the blazing sky, fusing with the sea in the heat. It was too hot to ruminate; the previous night's banquet had made him lazy anyway. But, scooping up sand in his right hand and letting it trickle between his fingers onto his bare chest as he squinted at the sky, he was startled by a vision—atoms, empty space. Then he fell asleep. Weeks later he recalled his vision. Perhaps Leucippus didn't even take his atoms very seriously, nor did his pupil Democritus, known as the laughing philosopher, because for him and his teacher atoms and empty space were merely a metaphor for the relative insignificance of creation. For their successors and their opponents the theory became a serious matter. Plato intellectualized Leucippus' vision, turning the atoms into an idea, which immediately lands us amid the problems posed by his theory of ideas, the labyrinth of a world constituted from concepts. Plato's atoms do not 'exist'—they underlie space and Becoming, they are imitations of existence, not ideas but shadows of the existence of ideas, the ultimate, fundamental geometric forms which explain the changes and the frailty of a world that does not 'exist' but merely partakes imperfectly of existence. Plato's atoms are similar and diverse; similar in the sense that they are isosceles, scalene or equilateral triangles, and diverse in the sense that they are of different sizes. Their similarity gives rise to the stability, their diversity creates the motion of the world that imitates existence—the two-dimensional atoms assemble themselves into regular three-dimensional bodies (a fabulous premonition of the molecule) which in turn make up the basic stereometric forms of the four elements from which Empedocles[4] believed the universe was formed: earth, water, fire and air. The basic forms of the element of earth are cubes, those of water are icosahedrons, those of fire are pyramids, those of air are octahedrons. These stereometric elements composed of atoms mingle, transform themselves and fill space such that no empty space (which exists only as an idea) exists, for space too is a likeness of existence, while the idea of empty space imitates or partakes of the idea of non-existence. (The contemporary theory of elementary particles seems almost concrete in comparison.) Leucippus' atomic vision is geometricized by Plato's atomic idea; neither of the two can be verified by experience but both have survived as intellectual models. Visions and ideas remain.

Plato spent his life grappling with the question of what ideas actually are. He sought permanence in them, immutability, what Parmenides called 'pure being'. The allegories in which he tried to intimate ideas are renowned, the 'Allegory of the Sun' and the 'Allegory of the Cave'. He was obsessed by a vision which he could not interpret. Plato's vision was the idea—the more concrete, the more helpless he became. In the tenth book of his *Republic*, Plato tried to demonstrate his idea about ideas by using chairs. The chair exists in three ways: as an idea, as a piece of furniture and as an imitation. As an idea the chair is eternal, its existence

4 Empedocles (*c*.490–430 BCE): Pre-Socratic Greek philosopher, originator of the theory of the four elements.

is perfect, it is 'produced' by God, as he puts it, and as an idea it can exist only once because 'we customarily hypothesize a single form in connection with each of the many things to which we apply the same name'.[5] If two chairs existed as ideas, these in turn could be traced back to one single chair as idea. God makes an idea only once. By contrast, the chair as a piece of furniture exists not only as a 'plurality' but in different variations as well, as a stool, footstool, armchair, etc. Underlying these chairs is the single form of their concrete plurality, the chair as an abstract idea; but the concrete chairs don't hold up for ever, there are risks involved in sitting on an antique wooden chair, if this ancient furniture still exists at all; the existence of chairs is transient and thus imperfect, the chairs on which we sit are made not by God but by people. Now, by the imitated chairs Plato means chairs in paintings. The painter does not make an ideal, eternal chair, like God, or a transient chair, like the joiner; he merely imitates, and not even the existence of the chair, at that, but only its appearance. And he has no other choice, for the existence of a chair, however imperfect, can be brought forth only by someone who manufactures a chair. The painter does not require this knowledge; he can depict a chair without being able to manufacture it. In contrast to the joiner's chair, the painter's picture partakes only of the chair's appearance, not of its existence. For example, a painter will depict a distant chair as smaller than a closer one, while someone who measures the chair will not succumb to this illusion; the measurements reflect the nature of the chair, not its appearance. The painter is an 'imitator . . . at the third remove from that which is'.[6] We

5 Plato, *Republic* (G. M. A. Grube trans., C. D. C. Reeve revd) (Indianapolis: Hackett, 1992), p. 265.

6 Ibid., p. 269.

have considerable difficulty with this line of reasoning. We are quite capable of being struck by creative notions for chairs but flounder when among all these notions for chairs we attempt to find the chair as abstract idea, as primal image, as primal chair. Does it have a back or not and, if so, does it have armrests? Does it have four legs or three or even just one, which would make the primal chair something like an abstract milking stool? Does the primal chair need legs at all; isn't even a tree stump almost a primal chair? Or are we looking in the wrong direction? Should we seek the primal chair among the noblest chairs, the thrones? Or among the most practical, the night stools, or even the most mobile, the wheelchairs, or in a chair that is at once throne, night stool and wheelchair? Is it a mistake to seek the primal chair among the chairs at all? Should the primal image of the chair be assumed to lie as an abstraction in the function of the chair, which consists in 'sitting more comfortably'; indeed, as this 'more comfortably' already expands on the possibility of sitting at all, doesn't even sitting contain the idea of the primal chair? But as something must seat itself in order to sit and as this something, to be able to sit, must possess something to sit with, Plato fares with the primal chair he wishes to sit on as I do with the audience I wish to address— the one recedes within him, the other within me, I don't need to go into detail. Both of us have failed. Plato sought to free language from the ambiguity with which the sophists played, making it into an unambiguous instrument of knowledge, and I sought to save language from the clichés which increasingly hem it in to such an extent that even a form of address becomes a problem. Now, of course Plato's failure is not the same thing as mine, the failure of a major power is not the same as that of a small business, but the two can very well founder on the same thing—the economy, for example, or, in the case of Plato and me, on language.

Both of us put too much strain on it. It collapsed beneath the weight we asked it to bear because it beguiled us into asking it to bear the weight that made it collapse—it was supposed to be more than just a language. I, to begin with the more harmless case, put a moral strain on language, asking it to be absolutely true at the expense of the convention with which no language can dispense. Nor with politeness. Language is communicative; its inaccuracies, ambiguities, erosions, abbreviations and not least its habits are conveyances for language debris, tempering terms and making them more tolerable, without them language does not flow. The art of speech consists in intimation, that of writing in writing between the lines. By contrast, Plato put language under an existential strain, asking not only that it be true, but that it be the truth. 'Small', 'large', 'beautiful', etc., are not unambiguous adjectives—an atom is extremely small but in relation to its nucleus extremely large, the earth is large compared with the moon and small compared with the sun, 'beautiful' is a subjective adjective. Plato transformed the terms 'smallness', 'largeness', 'beauty' into ideas, into primal forms of existing with respect to which something that is only relatively small, relatively large, relatively beautiful only partakes of existence, more non-existence than existence. But language too, in all its functions, is rooted in primaeval time. It evolved from cries of warning and joy, howls of triumph and lamentation, became informative but also magical; those who knew certain words, the secret names of gods, had power over life and death. Even Plato's assumption that language conceals existence, ideas, the essence of things, something absolutely objective, is ultimately magical, an outgrowth of thought from merely guessable primaeval times, and then again it points to our time, carrying forward mental possibilities. The assumption which he entertained in the end, that ideas are numbers, on the one hand points back to the Pythagoreans, who saw numbers as having qualities, and on the other hand antici-pates modern physics, for Plato saw his philosophy as a sci-ence, believing that he knew rather than merely opining, and he saw mathematics as the most certain knowledge without which there is no science—physics, too, is incon-ceivable without mathematics. Mathematics operates with pure concepts; we have no particular difficulties thinking a dimensionless point or a one-dimensional line because we simulate them, attributing no existence to them, pure con-cepts that they are. We meet with difficulties and bitter con-troversies only when we attempt to explain how we do this, in basic research. Man is capable of hitting his head against every wall, but he can also avoid walls. The point and the line are abstractions, while the point on paper observed through the microscope appears as a cluster of matter, and the straight line is also three-dimensional and not the least bit straight. For these reasons I fail to understand why a fourth or fifth dimension shouldn't be just as easy to imag-ine as the first and second, or none; all dimensions are deduced from the third, and it itself is an abstraction, a pure concept, an idea. Perhaps only mathematical ideas are ideas, which is why mathematics has something expansive about it. No bounds are set to its ideas, a perfected mathematics is unthinkable. Only in notation can mathematics be rendered purely, although the roots of notation lie in language. In his critique of Fichte's philosophy, Jean Paul distinguishes that which can be expressed in language from that which can only be thought; thus one could say that the notation of mathematics, as a technical aid, can only be translated back into the thinkable. The mental notation of mathematics is more abstract than abstract art could ever be. But precisely because physics attempts interpretation only with a view to mathematics, thus taking the risk of subordinating reality to mathematical ideas, its language is necessarily that of mathematics without physics being mathematics itself. Rather, its connection with mathematics imposes implacable bounds upon it—only what can be expressed mathematically is physical, the formal side of nature, nature as an idea.

Samuel Gagnebin, professor at the University of Neuchâtel, mathematician and thinker, a great authority on Spinoza, couldn't get over his astonishment, rereading *Timaeus* at the age of hundred and one, that Plato thought of atoms as two-dimensional triangles. 'Quelle drôle d'idée,'[7] he laughed. He was also hugely amused by Plato's story that the demiurge, after creating the world, the gods and the immortal souls, ordered the gods in turn to create mortal husks of plants, animal and human bodies, so that creation might be made imperfect, as perfection requires the imperfect as well. Plato's demiurge got tired, laughed Gagnebin, and when I retorted that the God of the Bible was clearly also exhausted after the six days of creating the world, otherwise he wouldn't have had to rest, he said: But he didn't fall asleep like Plato's demiurge, from whom nothing was ever heard since. Just to mention Plato's influence on Christianity, St Augustine could explain *Timaeus* only by hypothesizing that in Egypt Plato had learnt of the prophet Jeremiah. Plato's theory of the soul, his transplanting of Paradise, Purgatory and Hell from the myths to his cosmological concepts, etc., influenced Christianity far more than did Aristotle who provided the logical framework while Plato provided the imagination. But not only is Christianity a Platonic religion, Plato's influence on physics is also much greater than his supposition that ideas are numbers would lead one to believe. When Aristotle writes, 'The moving body comes to a standstill when the force which pushes it

7 'What a funny idea.'

along can no longer so act as to push it,'[8] he derives this theorem from observation—as soon as the soldiers stop pushing the siege engines of his pupil Alexander the Great, they remain stuck in the mud. But when Newton claims, 'Every body perseveres in its state either of being at rest or of moving uniformly straight forward, except insofar as it is compelled by impressed forces to change that state,'[9] this law is deduced not from an observation but from a conception. Newton imagined an ideal nature, imagined nature as an idea, as an abstract work of art, so to speak, the ground is perfectly flat, the wheels of the siege engine are perfectly round and consummately lubricated and the air is imagined away, the city it is meant to ram lies in infinity, so that the perfect plane which leads to it is infinite as well. Alexander needs no soldiers either, with his right hand he gives the enormous siege engine a perfunctory nudge, barely touching it, and propelled by the nudge the siege engine rolls evenly, in a straight line, towards the city. It is rolling still. It will roll for an eternity. The physicists think up a world in which the laws of nature appear. It is a Platonic world, only that the demiurge is man—not God. The natural laws he finds are not existent but, rather, indicate things that exist. They can therefore be verified or falsified while Plato's ideas can neither be refuted nor proven—Plato saw them as divine. An idea in physics must be dropped if it proves untenable. The ether, invisible, imponderable, and at the same time infinitely rigid, the medium in which light waves were supposed to travel and which would have explained

8 Cited in Albert Einstein and Leopold Infeld, *The Evolution of Physics* (Cambridge: Cambridge University Press, 1971), p. 6. The quote is said to stem from the *Mechanics*, erroneously attributed to Aristotle.

9 Isaac Newton, *Philosophical Writings* (Andrew Janiak ed.) (Cambridge: Cambridge University Press, 2004), p. 45.

the long-distance effect of gravitation, was proven to be unprovable by the ingenious Michelson-Morley experiment and hence abandoned. The Platonic ideas of physics are abstracted from reality and refuted or confirmed by experiments which in turn abstract reality. With his dialectical method, Plato distils from language pure concepts which vanish like gigantic but empty verbal bubbles in the intelligible world of his mind.

Then very different demiurges went to work—the technicians. They didn't interpret the world—they changed it. They were the tools of evolution, the true Karl Marxes, whom we credit, in primaeval times, not only with the mastery of fire but also with the invention of weapons, writing and money. And more than that. What the dinosaurs, the most successful living creatures to date, created from their skeleton throughout the many million years of their reign, altering their bones in ways that enabled the beasts to dominate the air, land and sea, humans create with the prosthetic world of their machines. They too are part of human biology; technology intertwines with human beings, becoming a part of them, of their bodies and their minds. Its basic ideas stem from science but once it has adopted an idea, creative notions come thick and fast. It has long since merged with science; none of the exact sciences can be imagined without it. The industrial landscape of CERN by Geneva, designed to locate particles predicted in theory, a major technical and scientific enterprise, over three thousand technicians, administrators, secretaries, physicists, plus guests, a huge operation, with governments in the wings, questions as to whether the whole thing is even financially sustainable, all of Europe is involved, the facility has already sprawled across the border, and yet all this is the result of a thought by a man who lay sleepily on the beach millennia ago, letting sand run through his fingers onto his bare chest, a vision that brains have filtered down the centuries until it became a model, then an increasingly complex construct, changing from a sort of planetary system to a fog, which ultimately can only be thought, only paraphrased with allegories, and at the same time has become a magical word, awe-inspiring like a magical word from primaeval times, as though the vision had survived thanks only to the magic that clung to it, so that people think it a sacrilege to divide the indivisible, and as I reflected on it and on the fact that the same man who was overcome by the vision of the atoms imagined, staring into the empty, blazing sky above him, that there is an empty space within the cosmos and an empty space outside the cosmos and that in the endless emptiness innumerable worlds form from countless atoms, the silent domes loomed over the pine forest of a mountain near San Diego, Mount Palomar. There were hikers with backpacks, just like in Switzerland. We were admitted in. The world's largest precision instrument, a reflecting telescope five yards in diameter, the Russians had a larger one, we were told, but thank God it had a crack and was unserviceable, though Mount Palomar was gradually becoming unserviceable as well, the lights from Los Angeles and San Diego pollute the night sky. Unlike at CERN, we met few people, the administrator, two astronomers, one technician, the other one was sleeping. They demonstrated the giant telescope for me, opened, then rotated, the dome. Something between a crane and an elevator lifted me seven or eight yards above the massive mirror, in the seat where Zwicky and Baade[10] once sat. 'God, if the director knew . . .' the technician muttered. Baade and Zwicky had spent entire nights observing

10 Fritz Zwicky (1898–1974): Swiss physicist and astronomer; Walter Baade (1893–1960): German astronomer and astrophysicist. They are known for their joint work on supernovas.

the sky, shivering in their winter coats beneath the open dome. Now everything was automated, no one had looked through the eyepieces for years; video cameras replaced the human eye, working nights alone under the open slit of the slowly turning dome. We entered an adjoining building. The Jupiter Symphony rang out to meet us. The astronomer sat at his computer, feeding in the data which the spectrograph had analysed overnight, numbers on a monitor, the recorded colour spectrogram already broken down into numbers. Another monitor showed the object which the cameras had recorded, it too already processed, a white expanse on which the stars, black dots, massed together in a lens-like forma-tion. A Seyfert galaxy, he said, barely to be heard, Mozart was so loud, and then he said, 'That's the fugue.' The Jupiter Symphony was over. The bored astronomer went on feed-ing data. 'I can't afford a secretary,' he said. I asked diffi-dently, as one who employs a secretary, whether what I had heard on Swiss radio just before my departure was true, that they had discovered a Milky Way incomparably larger than ours. 'No idea,' he said, explaining that he was only con-cerned with Seyfert galaxies, and put on the second G-minor symphony. Outside, I asked about the archive. Thousands of photographs, including Zwicky's famous first photo of a supernova in a distant galaxy. Suns, worlds, and again I had to think of Leucippus squinting up into the blazing sky. Surely he owned some slaves; the astronomer I had just left had only a few machines at his disposal, but what machines. The Greeks couldn't imagine a world without slaves, not even Plato could, and the slave existed as an idea too, as a God-created, abstract, eternal slave, and the state which he imagined as the idea of a state would, had he managed to establish it, and he tried it three times, have been a Hell, even if its purpose was to realize the good. But people meant nothing to him, not because he despised them but because he had divided them into significance and insignificance—not only into soul and body but also into significant and insignificant people, so that there were significant people with significant souls, for example, aristocrats and philosophers, and insignificant people with insignificant souls, for example, women and slaves. The idea meant everything to him, because man was transient, merely the image of his soul, and the soul alone was eternal, but it too was merely an image of the primal idea of the good, beautiful and true. It is a value. Science is value-free; how can its world, abstracted, run through cyclotrons and halls of mirrors, broken down into binary numbers, contain values; it is purely aesthetic, beautiful, but beyond good and evil. Yahweh blazed his Ten Commandments in modified cuneiform into two stone tablets cut from Mount Sinai. He was a personality, and what a personality, who set values with his commandments, and what values, he was integrated into the world, whereas in an expanding and exploding universe shot through by cosmic catastrophes a personal God is no longer imaginable, except perhaps as a world principle. Moses could wrestle with Yahweh, Job could struggle with him, you can love him, you can hate him, praise him or curse him; God as a world principle can be admired or imagined away. It leaves no void. There is no reason to assume it. Good and evil have become a human affair. But as I left Mount Palomar the suspicion came to me that the technicians' creative notions are Plato's ideas and that we are the images of these ideas. Who was actually exploring our world—the vast particle accelerator in Geneva or the physicists, the gigantic telescope on Mount Palomar or the astronomer? Who is dependent on whom, who is whose slave? I thought, walking towards the rental car as the G-minor symphony blared after me.

Science interprets, art represents; science aims at the unambiguous, art at the ambiguous; the former at the concept, the latter at the image; the one at the idea, the other at the vision. Science and art are not equivalent human creations but equal ones. Progress exists in both, in science because it is forced to produce ever-new interpretations, in art because technology provides it with ever-new possibilities. Not for nothing did the Greeks use the same word for art and technology. Just as modern science is inconceivable without photography, modern art is inconceivable without film. Though we may no longer be convinced by Plato's reasons, in his *Republic*, for wishing to expel Hesiod, Homer, the tragedians and comedians from his state as poetic imitators, namely that 'their works are . . . easily produced without knowledge of the truth (since they are only images, not things that are)',[11] one cannot ignore the fact that this introduces into art a concept which would long hold its own, though not in Plato's reproving sense—the concept of imitation (mimesis). Aristotle expanded on the notion of art as imitation: 'Epic poetry and Tragedy, Comedy also and Dithyrambic poetry, and the music of the flute and the lyre in most of their forms, are all in their general conception modes of imitation,'[12] he writes at the very beginning of his fragment *Poetics*. Even Carl Burckhardt[13] could write of Rembrandt's *Self-Portrait with Saskia*: 'It is enough to ask: What would become of this figure if she stood up?' And I question whether the discovery of perspective launched the 'scientific age', given that perspective in painting falls precisely under the concept of imitation. It is a device to represent three-dimensionality on a two-dimensional surface. Imitation is an unfortunate concept for

11 Plato, *Republic*, p. 269.

12 Aristotle, *Poetics*, p. 1.

13 Carl Jacob Christoph Burckhardt (1818–97): Swiss historian of art and culture, and an influential figure in the historiography of each field.

art. It was first breached by the new artistic possibilities created by photography and film; they liberate painting from mimicry. And not only it but photography and film themselves; precisely because these new media mastered imitation perfectly, they learnt how to represent, how to see human beings anew. Art confronts the world no less than does the thinker, it confronts the world with visions. Lear lost in the storm, the two wretched figures waiting for Godot, Stubb descending into the gigantic sperm whale cadaver to extract ambergris, Emilia forcing her father to kill her because he has no idea what temptation is, Federico Fellini's helpless journalist rowing across the sea, alone in a boat with a rhinoceros, with this symbol of our stubborn world. But the non-depictable becomes depictable as well. I am thinking not only of the *Paradise* of Bosch, of that funnel into space leading to an ever-more powerful brightness, to a space behind space, or of Piranesi, whose dungeons sprawl as though into four dimensions, I am thinking of my dead friend Varlin's leather armchair, in which he portrayed me and many others, until in one of his last pictures he portrayed only it, *My Armchair*. In fact it's two chairs he painted, for if you look closer you can make out another chair. While the leather chair is tattered and filthy, covered with paint and soaked with oil, it would be impossible for different reasons to sit on the second chair, so unreal in its perspective and yet painted with such peculiar accuracy, as though this flawed construction really existed. By contrast, above his leather armchair's mighty decay, a few hasty strokes of charcoal suggest a dresser. On this dresser lie several white lilies, clustered as though the full moon were breaking through dark clouds. They lend the armchair an air of definitiveness, finality, and it seems to me that in the unsuccessfully foreshortened chair in the background and in the mouldering leather armchair Plato's primal image of a chair is manifested, as though between these two chairs all the chairs in the world can be intuited as a possibility and, what is more, that Varlin's world of chairs is the world that will remain of us one day, the world of the exploded neutron bomb in which nothing is left but senseless things, no life, nothing but forms—which brings me back to Plato. I wrote my first term paper as a philosophy student about him, his criticism of the poets, and the allegory of the cave which begins Book 7 of the *Republic*, with the people shackled from childhood by the legs and necks, able only to stare at silhouettes on a wall, is one of the reasons I became a writer—to find allegories for the world. In the allegory of the cave, Plato is Kafka's great forerunner, depicting the boundary of the knowable just as Kafka depicted the cruelty of justice and the arbitrariness of grace in the god he was supposed to believe in. But Plato, the first modern writer, seeming to create everything from his intellect, managed still more than that. Without Plato, Socrates would have remained one case among many, a figure such as Diogenes, of undoubted interest for philologists, now and then brought to life on stage in Aristophanes' *Clouds*. It was Plato who made him into a figure of world stature, a man who had to drink the cup of hemlock because he would rather suffer injustice than do injustice, a man who knew that he knew nothing. Plato's art brings this man more and more into the present day, admonitory and not without irony, since we are in the process of becoming his parody. For if we are forced to drink the hemlock one day, it will only be because we prefer to do injustice than suffer justice and because we do not know that we know something.

Humanity's fate will depend on whether politics finally deigns to hold sacred every single life or whether the whore will keep walking the streets for those to whom nothing is sacred. The lady must make up her mind. The way she's used by the statesmen who matter today is a mockery that makes reason blush with shame and spells constant fear for all those ones who never matter—the other two billion people who inhabit this planet. The wilful injustice with which politics disregards the individual—in the eternal manner of fools viewing only abstractions as real, namely the nations, imputing to them all the motives the individual never has—ultimately prevents us from approaching it with indulgence and blandishments. Today the main thing is to understand none and grasp none of what goes on there; the folly of today's politics is all too clear. Nothing more can excuse how both sides play with the Third World War, for war is not only an insane crime, it is in equally great measure an act of foolishness. And so there are two things the individual can do today: learn the art of dealing with dinosaurs whose brains have always been the size of sparrows', and towards whom indulgence is never called for, only caution; and, say the truth, shout it if need be, as long as humanly possible, for the one to be warned, lurching up ahead, both blind and drunk, towards the abyss in whose depths a slaughterhouse now seems to glimmer, a mushroom cloud now seems to rise, is humanity, is us ourselves.

But there is no sense in protesting when it is unclear what you are protesting for. Humanity must know what is possible, what it can expect from the commonality and what only the individual can do. Otherwise it will want the impossible and run the risk of foundering upon the special interests of individuals or committing suicide from boredom, seeing war either as a cure-all or as an adventure, not to mention those who see it as a business, they speak for themselves. But the opportunities of a time are always just as great as the deadly peril that hangs over it. It is a platitude that reality and possibility diverge today as never before, but our time is second to none in flouting platitudes. As never before, there is the possibility of organizing the planet as a whole and creating fair living conditions for all, a task made all the more urgent as our consciousness now encompasses the Chinese farmer and the Argentine shepherd—we have moved closer together. But this requires a form of politics that at last becomes a science, rather than reaching for the stars. What today is a matter of the drive for power must become a matter of reason. It is no longer a question of organizing power centres and squabbling over borders—the task of politics must be staked out anew. Some expect everything from it while others expect nothing any longer. Some have made a metaphysics of it, others a business. The thing to make of it is a tool that protects people instead of raping and exploiting them. The task is to establish an economy whose dynamics are no longer derived from the fact that one segment of humanity lives in affluence while the other, overwhelmingly larger one, lives in abject poverty. The dance round the Golden Calf must be stricken from humanity's repertoire; the accompanying music is growing increasingly excruciating. But again and again come calls for an encore, and on other stages people are already dancing round new calves. The tasks of politics lie in the present, not the future; it is about us, not about the unborn grand-children in whose name today's are being killed. The mis-understandings are immense. The totalitarian states have cast suspicion on organizations by destroying the individual and the individuals have sown it in freedom by abusing this freedom. It must be clarified what is Caesar's and what is the individual's. Only thus can the opportunity of the peoples, which shrinks with the inevitable waning of the nationalist idea which buoyed them up, be redeemed by the opportunity of the individual which increases in equal measure.

The assertion borders on mockery at a time in which intellect is often a death sentence and what has chiefly increased is the individual's opportunity to lose his head. And yet, though still tentatively, a Ptolemaic turn is looming. Whereas hitherto the individual attempted to deduce his duty from a universal world view, or at least hoped to find such a world view one day and then revolve round it like the earth around the sun, now he becomes the centre once again, of necessity, for following the collapse of the philo-sophical systems the scientific system is collapsing as well; indeed, the signs are increasing that the sciences are unable to provide any world view at all. The world's mystery remains untouched. Today it is easier to believe in the Res-urrection than in the world view of dogmatic Marxism, with whose problems only the present day grapples, lagging far behind the latest knowledge, as always, and in the process of failing this examination too.

And so we as individuals are simultaneously powerless and powerful. History seems to unfold without our assis-tance, yet mysteriously there are strings we can pull. The possibility of faith is intact, and the school of science has honed our judgement. We are gifted with greater qualifica-tions, as it were. The future of humanity is uncertain, but we can still seize the moment. Peace will be hard, be it the peace that follows a long war or the one without this detour, for peace means everyday life, and the everyday, the ordinary, the humdrum will only increase. Our intensity will decide whether the goods of this earth are transformed in our hands into gold or to dust. Less and less will humanity be able to afford adventures of the old kind, it will return disappointed from flights to the moon; new adventures must be found and they will be those of the mind. In the best-case scenario, politics will establish secure social spaces, to illuminate which will be the task of the individual; otherwise the earth will become a prison. An organization is forced to schematize; only the individual is capable of taking Ivan more seriously than the Soviet Union and thus restoring the true scale of things. From politics we must demand reason, from the individuals love. It is the task of politics to ensure that the opportunities of a few individuals become individual opportunity.

ON TOLERANCE

1977

FOREWORD AFTER THE FACT

I abandoned my philosophy studies in 1946 with the official excuse of becoming a painter and the secret intention of becoming a writer. Since then I have occupied myself with philosophy mainly because, as a producer of literature, literature bores me, but often driven as well by the slight sense of guilt at having absconded from philosophy. Not to overrate my studies, however—I was a pretty lazy student. In my high-school days I read Schopenhauer and Aristotle more like novels. As students we had to grapple with Plato and Aristotle, which we did by boning up on the Windelband and, in a pinch, the Compact Schwegler.[1] In my last year at the university a lecturer appeared who tried to make us warm to Heidegger's existentialism. My lingering animosity towards Heidegger must stem from this time. My dissertation was supposed to be on 'Søren Kierkegaard and the Tragic'. Nothing came of it. But Kierkegaard continued to unsettle me. Even my father engaged with his work. For some time I've been preoccupied by the *Unscientific Postscript* (1846), which I regard as Kierkegaard's most

Acceptance speech for the Buber-Rosenzweig Medal, 6 March 1977.

1 Standard histories of philosophy by the German neo-Kantian Wilhelm Windelband (1848–1915) and the theologian and philosopher Albert Schwegler (1819–57) respectively.

important work. I never got on with Hegel. Even with the greatest of optimism I could never share his view that world history is the realization of the Spirit, unless this Spirit is extraordinarily bloodthirsty. What Hegel wrote is a dramaturgy which he imputed to history. As a dramaturgy, it is irrelevant to historical reality; like every dramaturgy, it is a matter of aesthetics. Thus Hegel's effect on those who equate aesthetics with reality. (To a large extent the historians' methodological dispute strikes me as a dispute among dramaturges. They're all novelists, Leopold von Ranke to my mind the greatest among them, provided one is able to forget, while reading, that he too fancied himself a chronicler.) But again and again I made the effort to find meaning in Hegel. The most recent was 1970–71. Condemned to a seven-week hotel stay due to a directing job, I swore to myself that I would read the entire *Phenomenology of Spirit* (1807). It was to be a false oath. I made it only as far as the realization of rational self-consciousness through itself, at which point the undertaking seemed too irrational. I saw no pleasure or necessity in tackling the chapter 'Pleasure and Necessity' either. I gave up. All right, that's my fault, not Hegel's. Back in my student days I'd fared no better with his *Logic* (1812–16). His self-moving concepts, this formidable self-transformation of Being into Nothing and Nothing into Becoming, etc., seemed to me nothing more than a desperate juggling of concepts, a careening about in the prison of language. Fichte's dialectic (whose method Hegel adopted), proceeding from the I rather than from the concept, still strikes me as the more important of the two— it hints at the existential and ethical problem of how the individual reaches the neighbour, and by way of the neighbour reaches society, whereby Fichte can admittedly be interpreted differently, for his 'I' signifies not the individual, but the 'objective I', the 'mathematical point which does not exist at all', as Kierkegaard calls it and to which he objects. But German idealism interested me only insofar as I saw it as a constant, desperate attempt to somehow keep practising metaphysics after Kant. Hence the attempts, including Schopenhauer's, to figure out the 'thing in itself'. What most preoccupied me as a student, and has stayed with me since, was the *Critique of Pure Reason*. Of subsequent importance for me: Hans Vaihinger's *Philosophy of As If* (1911), Arthur Eddington's brilliant *Philosophy of Physical Science* (1939), Alexander Wittenberg's *Denken in Begriffen* (Thinking in Concepts, 1957) and finally, of course, Karl Popper. Though now he ought to follow *The Open Society and Its Enemies* (1945) with a work on 'The Open Society and Its Consequences'.

All this is not to pass me off as a thinker, any more than I would ascribe to the following lecture a philosophical value which it does not and cannot have—I was concerned only with making political points on the basis of my thinking. But it is necessary to indicate the intellectual environment one comes from, however much in it may be unresolved or false. And, to clarify my position still further—my relationship towards theology is strained, for as a pastor's son I have a natural aversion to all that is theological. All the more reason to engage with it. I owe much to theology, albeit to its contrary impulses. Karl Barth's[2] *Epistle to the Romans* (1922) was a revolutionary book for me and his *Dogmatics* (1932–67), which I often read, a mathematical masterpiece. The passages on Judaism are taken from it, from Volume 1, Part 2, and Volume 3, Part 3. The passage on Hegel is drawn from his *Protestant Theology in the Nineteenth Century* (1947). The Kierkegaard quotes are taken from the edition *Unwis-*

---

2 Karl Barth (1886–1968): Swiss Protestant theologian, one of the twentieth century's most important Christian thinkers.

senschaftliche Nachschrift (Unscientific Postscript) (Cologne: Jakob Hegner, 1959), pp. 337–8. At the end I cite Popper several times, from *Objektive Erkenntnis* (Objective Knowledge) (Hamburg: Hoffmann und Campe, 1973).[3] Hegel's words on the true form of truth can be found in his *Phenomenology*. I also used three statements by Mao Zedong, who, as he himself claimed, was once a Kantian. A pity, really, that he didn't remain one.

Ladies and Gentlemen,

That the German Coordinating Council of Societies for Christian-Jewish Cooperation has awarded me the Buber-Rosenzweig Medal came as a twofold surprise for me—I knew of the existence of neither the medal nor the council.

3 These volumes are available in English as:

Karl Barth, *Church Dogmatics*, VOL. 1, *The Doctrine of the Word of God*, PART 2 (G. T. Thompson and Harold Knight trans) (London and New York: T&T Clark, 1956).

Karl Barth, *Church Dogmatics*, VOL. 3, *The Doctrine of Creation*, PART 3 (G. W. Bromiley and R. J. Ehrlich trans) (London and New York: T&T Clark, 1960).

Karl Barth, *Protestant Theology in the Nineteenth Century: Its Background and History* (Brian Cozens and John Bowden trans) (Grand Rapids, MI: William B. Eerdmans, 2002[1959]).

Søren Kierkegaard, *Concluding Unscientific Postscript to the Philosophical Fragments* (Howard V. Hong and Edna H. Hong trans) (Princeton, NJ: Princeton University Press, 1992).

Karl R. Popper, *Objective Knowledge: An Evolutionary Approach* (London: Oxford University Press, 1972).

G. W. F. Hegel, *Phenomenology of Spirit* (A. V. Miller trans.) (London: Oxford University Press, 1977).

As though intuiting my ignorance, this council recently sent me the preamble to its statutes, which states among other things that the societies' work, with mutual respect for all differences, focuses particularly on the relationship between Christians and Jews, a relationship which for many members is characterized by a shared belief in the God of Revelation; that these societies also take a public stand for people with different world views, for active cooperation between Christians and Jews and for the fostering of cordial relations with the state of Israel; and finally, that ideological fanaticism, religious bigotry, racial discrimination, social oppression and political intolerance threaten the moral and physical existence of the individual and of entire groups and peoples.

Ladies and gentlemen, I neither know when this preamble was written nor who wrote it. I imagine that it dates back to 1952 at the latest, as the last dying gleam of a time when people still believed in a new religious, moral and political beginning, an inward and an outward one, yet a time already shadowed by the fear that this new beginning might fail to materialize. This fear was not unfounded. On one side democracy had been reintroduced but the entanglement between the guilty and the guiltless, the collaborators and the victims was too great, and the incipient economic miracle, which people are already mourning, forgetting that it was made possible chiefly by the unique political situation that followed the defeat, this meteoric launch into a prosperity unequalled before or after threatened to sweep everything along with it—the state, the parties, the cultural institutions and the churches; while on the other side Prussia was reborn, not in spirit, admittedly, but in its discipline.

The fears proved founded. The new beginning failed to materialize. For the vanquished and for the victors, who saw their victory as proof that their political systems were the only true ones, suddenly setting truth against truth, system against system. The neutral parties, too, believing they had passed the examination, neglected to examine themselves. Indeed, what threatened the Jews once German anti-Semitism had shaped them into a people—extinction—now threatened what this people had established for itself by natural law—its state.

If we ask ourselves with heavy hearts what insights the world actually gained from the Second World War, there is only one uneasy answer—since then, two different actors have played the main roles and another has already taken over the third; those who previously played main roles now perform supporting parts, whether they were among the victors or the vanquished. Indeed, many who were victims once have remained victims, preyed on by one, then the other. Certainly, the ranks of the extras have swelled immeasurably, the scenery is on a grand scale, the props are more terrifying, the stage equipped with unprecedented technical refinements, with better lighting than ever, and a thunder machine that can destroy stage and actors in one fell swoop. But it's the same play, with the same accusations and ripostes. The same plot unfolds before us, always starting anew and yet always unfolding the same way. Only the number of victims constantly increases. The dramaturgy of world history seems not to have changed, nor even the speculations on the nature of this dramaturgy. Some still assert that it progresses with rigorous logic—whoever exits the stage is wrong, whoever enters it is right, until he himself is forced to exit. Others are still of the opinion that it demonstrates the progress of reason. Others believe what they believed in before—in the class struggle that constitutes the dramaturgy of the play. Still others see in it what they have always seen—the demonstration that back in the olden days all was well with the world and that world history, which has become worse and worse ever since, must finally find its way back to the source. Some see it as God's judgement, some as the self-judgement of humanity. But most simply resign themselves; the dramaturgy of world history consists for them of chance inspirations, crazy gaffes and slips of the tongue, collapsing backdrops, stages revolving out of control, absurd motivations and grotesque plots.

If that were so, the preamble would be pointless, seeking only to ban the contrivances required to drive the plot we call world history, without which it could not happen at all. But even if we imagine a meaningful, rather than an absurd, dramaturgy of world history—for example, as the realization of Spirit—the preamble seems at most to represent the goal to which world history, in this best of all possible cases, would aspire. For how, say, could class struggle be conducted with political tolerance, without the ideological fanaticism which, after all, goes along with the conviction that class struggle is necessary—indeed, without the social oppression which appears as its natural cause?

It could also be, however, that the dilemma in which the preamble places us lies in the very notion that world history is determined by some sort of dramaturgy. Perhaps the dramatic course of world history has merely seduced us into suspecting a dramaturgy behind it. Perhaps the parable of the sower who went out to sow is a more felicitous image— some seeds bore fruit, some a hundredfold, some sixtyfold, some thirtyfold, some were choked by thorns, some found too little soil, some were eaten by the birds, depending on the ground where the wind chanced to take them. Applying this parable of the Kingdom of God to world history, we take the sower to mean the human being and the ground on which the seeds fall to mean the nature sadly inherent in human beings in all their perversity, savagery, lethargy, complacency, in all their greed and lust for power and in their whole unconsciousness. But what do the seeds mean?

We must first ask whether the demand of the preamble means that the sower sows *different* seeds, some curbing ideological fanaticism, some making religious tolerance bloom, some preventing social oppression, etc., so that the preamble would be nothing but a noble organization's noble wish list of noble fruits; or, alternatively, whether the sower sows the *same kind* of seeds, so that when we speak of tolerance, for example, we also come to social justice.

Having ventured the attempt, having taken tolerance as a starting point, we find that *religious tolerance* seems to be prevailing across the boards. Even in Northern Ireland and in Lebanon religious motives seem to conceal political ones. In the first case it is a politically oppressed minority and in the second the annihilation of a people, the Palestinians, by a non-Christian power, the Syrians, backing a Christian power; on the other hand, if the Syrians back the Palestinians again—if they still exist as a power in Lebanon —the Christian Arabs will be annihilated.

And so it is *political tolerance* which is called into question everywhere to a greater or lesser degree, even in the democracies, by the plague of informers, by snooping into people's political views, by the 'Decree against Radicals',[4] by business wheelings and dealings. In a democratic country, it ought to be unthinkable for a party—which claims to be Christian and socially conscious—to conduct an election campaign under the slogan 'Freedom or Socialism', as though freedom and socialism were antinomies rather than necessary political guidelines which must both be borne in mind, as though a rational person could take socialism in

---

4 Controversial West German law from 1972 banning 'radicals' (mainly communists) from the civil service.

today's usage to mean dogmatism rather than the no-longer-deferrable necessity of enforcing justice, at least in the economic realm, as the sole prerequisite of the freedom that is still possible. Meanwhile, no one is surprised at religious tolerance any more. Even the Eastern Bloc, which has always been anti-Semitic to the core, resists being seen as anti-Semitic, resorting to the claim that it is merely anti-Zionist, while in the relationship of the Arabs to the Jews and the Jews to the Arabs, where it's right against right and shrine against shrine, political intolerance constantly threatens to poison religious tolerance—and religious intolerance political tolerance.

Given this fact, it is becoming increasingly urgent to come to an understanding on the nature of tolerance, for the term is ambiguous. It makes us particularly suspicious as the religions hit upon the notion of tolerance only after losing their power, not when they were in power, not to mention the intolerance of their own different tendencies. The 'religions of revelation' applied tolerance—when they applied it at all—in the literal sense of the word. When they were in power, they tolerated the others at best; since the Jews were never in power, tolerance acquired a purely passive meaning for them. The arrogance of the others, whether Christians or Muslims, was something they had to humbly suffer, not just tolerate, how and to the point of what atrocities need not be elaborated here.

As far as I can see, it was Lessing who first developed a new concept of tolerance. The dispute among the religions is senseless. There is no authority that can decide it. The judge is summoned and declares himself incapable of recognizing the true ring, the true religion; the believers' intolerance renders them suspect; all of them are 'deceived deceivers'. The judge in the famous ring parable can only advise each to live according to his religion, abide by its dictates, fulfil its spirit. Tolerance is a proposal for religious coexistence. Just as political coexistence does not suspend ideological differences, this coexistence does not suspend differences of belief, it simply ceases to call them into question. Lessing's tolerance is a wise move in an age which increasingly casts doubt on the religion of revelation but which still needs it as an ideology; the rulers govern by the grace of God.

In 1781, the year of Lessing's death, Kant published *The Critique of Pure Reason*. Refuting the proofs of God's existence is more than an act of logic. God recedes into the unprovable. He must necessarily be thought, but without ever being able to become the object of experience, evidently as a kind of necessary fiction. Theology is divorced from philosophy; the theologian has no place in philosophy and the philosopher none in theology. Knowledge becomes knowledge, belief becomes belief. But—thinking things further—this makes belief a private affair, the affair of the individual.

Kierkegaard thought things further. No oppression, no persecution ever called into question the Christian church, as did Kierkegaard's revolution, this attack from the standpoint of the individual. Persecution made it stronger, the Reformation sundered yet renewed it, the alliance with the State corrupted it. Kierkegaard's attack made the Church as institution a fiction, Christianity inwardness—a word I choose not because Kierkegaard chose it but because it has become discredited, not only politically, not only literarily, but, it seems, theologically as well. For some inwardness is a cosy, sentimental thing, for others something merely pietistic, ecstatic, at best mystical, and the politicians regard it as socially irrelevant. But for Kierkegaard inwardness is the fate of the human being, for no one can be *more* than one single individual and thus there can be no system for the inward, the existential, the essential. For the individual, subjectivity is the last thing he is left with and objectivity is what vanishes, the identity of thinking and being a chimera of abstraction. Only if the existing person could truly be outside himself would truth achieve completion for him; but Kierkegaard considers this impossible. Only for moments, he believes, can the single individual transcend existence as an existing person—in moments of passion.

And so one can say that Socrates' true pupil is not Plato but Kierkegaard. Like the Greek, he believes that all knowledge that does not pertain to existence is essentially chance knowledge, its degree and extent essentially indifferent. Kierkegaard's work is a personal testimonial; not *what* he thought is important but *how* he thought, believed, doubted, loved. And it is because of this, because of the passion of this individual who wanted to be nothing but an individual, who wanted not to proclaim but only to profess, that his *how* has become so crucial that this 'how something became known' takes us to a new 'what is to be known'. In the world of individuals, tolerance becomes existential. This seems paradoxical at first glance, for Kierkegaard's thinking is, by its approach, an attack on Hegel's thinking, who affirms the very thing which Kierkegaard so passionately denies—the truth of the identity of thought and being, to speak with Kierkegaard.

In Barth's interpretation, this identity is persistently upheld because it is based on the identity of confidence in God and confidence in the self, which is why the result of such thinking is a system, a perfectly tallied account of knowledge and balance of truth. On the basis of this identity, he argues, Hegel could—and had to—present himself as the man who implicitly knows everything and is authorized to summon everyone before his judgement seat. Barth even finds that all that appears to make up theology's special splendour and majesty is infinitely better preserved and honoured in Hegel's philosophy than in the hands of the theologians themselves (except perhaps Thomas Aquinas). Here theology, sustained and preserved in the act of philosophy, is not transcended but transcends itself.

I do not cite these words to show how one great dialectician takes the measure of another great dialectician; I am concerned with characterizing Kierkegaard's lonely intellectual endeavour. Kierkegaard does not attack details of Hegel's thinking, does not try to take him as a starting point or reinterpret him, as, for example, Schopenhauer does with Kant. For Kierkegaard, Hegel's philosophy is an impossibility as such. For him the identity of thinking and being is, as he says of the objective I, an accord in the cloud, an unfruitful embrace, and the relation of the individual I to this mirage is never stated. In Kierkegaard's eyes, Hegel's philosophy of the self-realizing thought is a senseless speculation of fantastical thinking, worth combating only insofar as it claims to be objective truth. Indeed, we must ask whether Kierkegaard's attack on Hegel is not an attack on philosophy as a whole. For what philosophy does not aim to deal in objective truth, and—we must add—what theology does not aim to do the same? For whether or not it wants to, in some way—however demythologized—it must take the Bible, the Word of God or tradition to be something objectively true. But then, from the perspective of philosophy and theology, one could counter Kierkegaard by asking whether the person who retreats to inwardness, summarily declaring all objective philosophical and theological knowledge to be impossible, is not in fact the intolerant one? What, one might further ask, is the point of all the talk about a supposed existential tolerance? Isn't this tolerance just as much hot air as the supposedly subjective truth which can at most be verisimilitude, a verisimilitude which, one cannot deny, even a lunatic's mad train of thought possesses; for verily, he too takes his thoughts to be true. But now I must admit that it exceeds my intellectual capacities to play the objective arbiter in Kierkegaard's dispute with Hegel. I merely speculate that Kant's refutation of the ontological proof of God —which infers God's existence from the concept of God — already refutes Hegel. A concept does not lose a single one of its characteristics by lacking existence, and thus Hegel, by ascribing being to his thought in order to make a metaphysics out of logic, resembles the merchant who—as Kant relates—improves his standing by adding a few zeroes to his bank balance.

But even if it seems to me that Kierkegaard is right about Hegel, Hegel has nonetheless emerged the victor. His philosophy proved more potent than its refutation. That the true form in which truth exists can only be its scientific system is Hegel's all-too-seductive description of all the systems which followed him and which made the same claim—political, philosophical and theological systems. Hegel is more than a German misfortune. For if something contradicts such a system, it must necessarily be false for this system. And as every such system wishes to be understood as universal, it is confronted again with the problem of tolerance in its original sense, assuming it does in fact confront it. Political systems of this kind can evade the issue, Barth cannot. For him as a Christian, the fact that the Bible as testimony to the humanity of God's revelation is simultaneously a testimony of the Jewish spirit represents the hardest test of Christian belief. Though Barth regards the existence of the Jewish people as the only natural proof of God's existence, he is forced to describe Israel as the people of God that has rejected God. For Barth, all later forms of anti-Semitism pale to insignificance beside this accusation. It speaks to Barth's truthfulness and plain-spokenness that he dares to speak the way he is forced to, as a dogmatist, as the herald of a theological system which for him, too, manifests the true form in which truth exists. Accordingly, for Barth it is only by the grace of God that a Christian can escape being an anti-Semite. This view may shock us but the scandal remains that one of the main roots of anti-Semitism lies in Christianity. It is to Barth's credit that he has spoken clearly here, and the same is true of every Jew who speaks just as clearly of his standpoint. But when Barth finds that Christianity's guilt lies in the fact that to this day it has failed to impress Israel as witnesses to the fulfilment of the Old Testament Word of God, since the Church as a whole has failed to make a persuasive impression upon the Jews in this regard, and when he speculates that perhaps the Jewish question will not be solved until the end of all things, as the eschatological resolution of this greatest of riddles, then Barth's tolerance is again that of Lessing—as in the Ring Parable, only in 'a thousand thousand years' will a judge decide which ring is the true one.

Existential tolerance argues differently—the Christian thinks of the Jew, God has revealed himself differently to him than to me; of the atheist, God has concealed himself from him. An atheist thinks of the Jew or the Christian, something persuades him that does not persuades me. But if we argue along these lines, the question of tolerance arises in yet a new sense: Does this tolerance now hold in the realm of politics as well?

Of course a staunch anti-Marxist can understand that someone else is a staunch Marxist and vice versa. But does existential tolerance still exist if one of the two is in power? Does tolerance exist between the powerful and the powerless, and—asking further—between the propertied and the non-propertied, or whichever social or political antagonisms we assume, does an existential tolerance exist between them?

There are those individuals who accept their powerlessness and their poverty. Indeed, the vast majority of people still dully accept their powerlessness or poverty or have resigned themselves once more. But to turn this tolerance around, to demand, say, that the powerful tolerate the powerless and the possessors the dispossessed, has something shocking about it. For that would be to demand that the powerless be left in their powerlessness and the dispossessed in their poverty, unless the powerful and the possessors decide to give up their power and their possessions for the sake of the powerless or the dispossessed—who, however, clearly cannot tolerantly make this demand if the powerful and the possessors are not persuaded. And how can they be persuaded?

At this point one can either capitulate or think things further. If the individual capitulates, he tolerates the world as it is, he endures it; if he accepts himself as its victim, shunted about by circumstances, he cannot get beyond existential tolerance, which throws him back upon himself. He must tolerate political intolerance and all that the preamble takes a stand against. If he thinks things further, from himself to his neighbour and from him to his neighbour and so on, driven by his conscience, he will realize that the individual—and thus each individual—is existentially powerless and existentially dispossessed, because if power and possessions fall to the individual—whether by an accident of birth or on the basis of certain abilities—they do so owing only to a political and economic system. And what political system is not simultaneously political and economic? The individual is then forced to call into question every system that privileges or oppresses individuals. Indeed, he cannot rest until he has found a just political system. For what the individual is capable of recognizing is the ethical, the justice that bears on the relationship of the individual to the individual—paradoxically, he must now posit this justice to be absolute, as Hegel does with the Spirit. But his inwardness, too, becomes possible only when he is able to free himself of his concerns about other individuals, in the sense that the social order becomes a matter of indifference to him because it has become just and thus merely necessary, posing no threat to existential things. But as the individual can never have the certainty that the world is just—without eliminating the others from his conscience— he becomes a paradox. He becomes a rebel whose sole power is his powerlessness. For the moment the individual reaches for power, he ceases to be an individual, his right to rebellion is suspended, since power is possible only within a system. The individual protests against the world but he cannot get beyond this protest, as an individual he is a protest. If he wants to be more than a protest, if he wants revolution instead of rebellion, he must confront power with power, one system with another system.

But this takes us from Kierkegaard to Marx and his mission—to make freedom possible for the person, the individual, to lead him from the realm of necessity to the realm of freedom. Takes us back, actually. Like Kierkegaard, Marx also attacked Hegel, turning him on his head when he meant to put him on his feet. This created the most potent political weapon ever invented, but Marx had reached a dead end, for by adopting Hegel's logic he too had to see his system as the true form in which truth exists. He did proceed from the idea of realizing the free individual and, unlike Hegel, did not move from the individual to the idea, to the absolute Spirit, but because he merely turned Hegel on his head, the navel stayed where it was. The objective Spirit, the State in Hegel, the Party in Marx, the dictatorship of the proletariat are identical. Indeed, the Marxists now in power have long since turned Marx on his head. And so the old Hegelian police state is resurrected, just unimaginably more powerful than in Hegel's Prussia.

The reason is easily discerned. Because the entire system is burdened by the claim to truth, the idea from which it proceeds must become a true idea, an ideology, the only true Church out of which—like it or not—the only true State crystallizes because no more progress is possible. The goal, the freedom of the individual, becomes illusory. This is the only explanation for the mindless intolerance of these structures. They understand political tolerance as Lessing does religious tolerance—as different political tendencies coexisting side by side but not, as in Lessing, interpenetrating each other. Woe to the one in their ranks who demands the civil rights they endorsed in Helsinki.[5] What they endorsed, in their view, is that we may have civil rights according to our conviction and they may have theirs according to their ideology. It is not the human rights that hold but their interpretation; thus they become relative. But the right to opposition is an existential right of the individual. It is absurd to accuse him of intolerance towards an intolerant political system and thrust him forcibly into the position of the individual—into that of the outcast. For the position of the individual is a position of freedom, not of force. There is also such a thing as a freedom of the prisoner, but only a prisoner may speak of it. In the mouth of a prison warden these words are blasphemy.

5 Reference to the Helsinki Accords of 1975, which sought to improve relations between the Eastern Bloc and the West.

But for all that we must not forget the mission of one such as Karl Marx—the freedom of the individual can only be the freedom of all. This should be the mission of our political system as well. Often, it only appears to be. We want none of economic democracy. Participation is declared to be a priori impossible. The freedom of the spirit, oppressed in the East because they believe in the truth of their system, is something we permit only to prove the truth of our system. Freedom, a nuisance for the East, is an alibi for the West—that is exaggerated, but it is our time that exaggerates it.

What is to be done? What political conclusions must we draw as individuals? Above all, surely, that we need a new Age of Enlightenment, that we must drop from our political systems the claim to truth, justice and freedom and replace it with the search for truth, justice and freedom, with rationality. We must examine how rational our political systems are. I am not so sure that we would come off better than the East. Its rationality consists in taking a false principle for the truth and stubbornly enforcing it while our irrationality consists in stubbornly applying rationality irrationally. But what is rationality that is conceived not as truth but as a search for truth, justice and freedom?

Hegel has been refuted not only by Kierkegaard but also by modern science, by the fact that it arrived at something which Hegel did not attain, though he thought he had attained it—objective knowledge. And science arrived at this knowledge because its logic is not Hegel's. He finishes off philosophy. He is its formal but not its essential culmination. His logic is irrelevant to scientific thinking. Mao's phrase that all things have inherent contradictions and it is they that make up the movement and development of these things could also be from Marx or Hegel. Scientifically speaking, it is nonsense. The contradictory nature of things lies in the way a person understands them. The Ptolemaic and Copernican interpretations of the solar system do not constitute contradictions within the solar system but, rather, a wrong and a more correct view of this system. By eliminating errors, the logic of science leads to objective knowledge, to progress. In Hegel, truth arises mechanically, from a kind of technique with which the Spirit realizes itself. One truth begets another which stands in contradiction to the first. But the contradiction is not disruptive; both are equally true, because each age has its Spirit which produces the truth of its age, until the process is crowned by the system of the contradiction-free absolute truth of the Absolute Spirit—for Hegel in the Hegelian system, for Marx in the classless society. This is the logic of an Absolute Spirit, incarnated in the course of history. By contrast, the logic of science is that of the creative person. Hegelian logic is unprovable; scientific logic leads to proofs which can be confirmed or refuted. But for this very reason it is irrational to discard the very aspect of Marx which holds up to the judgement of scientific logic—the insight into techniques of human exploitation. How that takes place is also important to know. Marx's system should be abandoned, its scientific insights used. There is also a rational tolerance—rationality tolerates what is rational. Only here it barely makes sense to speak of tolerance any more. It becomes self-evident.

But if we subordinate our politics to a rationality thus understood, to a rationality which dares to eradicate the errors it made, the errors which led to ideological fanaticism, religious bigotry, racial discrimination, social oppression and political intolerance, our states too will be transformed from the mythical constructions which they are increasingly becoming into the institutions which they should be, institutions that are increasingly capable of improvement, which they can only be if they can be constantly criticized, assessed and changed, so that they become constructions towards which we can let ourselves be tolerant—in the active sense—so that we can endure them. I know we shiver when we hear of institutions. But if science is a grand adventure of the mind, aiming not at the discovery of absolutely certain theories but at the invention of ever-better theories which can be subjected to ever-stricter tests, as Popper puts it, we should discover this adventure for our institutions too, applying it to them by making them more and more just and rational, by seeing them not as systems of compulsion but as works of art that exist for the sake of humanity, not humanity for their sake.

Under such conditions it would be much easier not only to realize the preamble of the German Coordinating Council but also to guarantee, at last, the existence of the state of Israel. Indeed, even the existence of a Palestinian state would be possible. Albeit with two misgivings. The history of humanity is not an uninterrupted forward development from the realm of necessity into the realm of freedom; rather, it is a march into the realm of ever-greater necessity. Constantly growing, humanity falls under the law of large numbers. This law is implacable—it will make humanity poorer. This law will revoke freedoms and privileges which today we still see as inviolate, for it means that in the political, in the economic, even in the technological realm the search for justice must come before the search for freedom. A humanity becomes thinkable for which there is but one freedom left—intellectual freedom. Kierkegaard's individual, the inward person, will then become identical with the free person as understood by Marx. But without tolerance this world would become a hell. Indeed, even with this tolerance —if politics plays out this way—a person can survive only if he possesses the inner resources to suffer himself and his neighbour. War is easier to bear than peace. The peace imposed by the law of large numbers will be the hardest of all to bear. Really, I should have spoken of that, of the wisdom of living in peace with oneself and one's neighbour, of this highest form of tolerance. But I cannot speak of it. Not only because I lack this wisdom in many ways but because only self-evident things can be spoken of. But the most self-evident thing is rationality, if we are speaking of people, and only of them can we speak. But this is just where it turns difficult again, if not impossible, for rationality is always confused with common sense, which animals possess to such a greater degree and which, in people, is so good at applying rationality irrationally.

And so there is one last thing I fear—that the seed of rationality has long since yielded fruits but blighted ones, for it fell on poor ground; that the states have become mighty institutions, have ossified as such, their ground long since paved over so that no new seed can flourish, and now—like dead churches—are equipped with a vast clergy disguised both as government and opposition, or as the almighty Party; that all struggles are personal power struggles, unconcerned with improving this construction; that the practitioners of power, seeking to cover themselves and their struggles, ring the bells and attempt to justify these deserted cathedrals anew with the belief that these institutions are fatherlands, not with a good belief, though, but with the most terrible—with the fear of a potential enemy, within and without. But he who sows fear reaps weapons. Not just a good business but a deadly one. And so the world bristles with weapons. We are delivered up to this world, believers and unbelievers, all peoples, the state of Israel and all states. For the terrible thing about fear is that it creates a reality which justifies it retroactively. To have no fear in this world may be *the* message which we can receive not from rationality but from that mysterious human ability which—somewhat sheepishly—we call belief.

Ladies and gentlemen, I thank the German Coordinating Council of Societies for Christian-Jewish Cooperation for the Buber-Rosenzweig Medal. It forced me to think about the council's preamble. I am sorry that my speech turned out so long. But so it is—you can't simply get away with giving me a medal. For I have ventured this speech only because I am not really a thinker but someone who just lets loose. You are the ones who let me loose at you.

ABU KHANIFA AND ANAN BEN DAVID

1975

Theologians don't always get off more lightly. Their teachings, too, have explosive potential. Here Judaism and Islam display yet another commonality which seems to lie in the nature of theology. Each based on a 'revealed' scripture, neither religion is content with its revelations. Just as the Jews expand on the Bible with the Talmud, a dialectical commentary on the Pentateuch, the Muslims supplement the Koran with the Sunna and Hadith, the oral tradition of the deeds and words of the Prophet. Around 760 CE, the Abbasid al-Mansur has the theologian Abu Khanifa arrested—having, as the Prophet's official successor, got into a vexing theological dispute with the great Koran expert—and annoyed at theologians in general, he commands, before withdrawing, reluctant but dutiful, from the daily affairs of the state to his harem, that a rabbi by the name of Anan ben David should be cast into the dungeon as well. No one dares to ask al-Mansur why; perhaps he doesn't know himself. Perhaps he is merely acting on a vague sense of that malicious righteousness that distinguishes the caliphs as rulers over believers and unbelievers alike. But it's also possible that he dimly remembers having skimmed a petition, though unaware where this petition came from, whether from an office in his administration that deals with Jewish affairs or even from several offices, in fact it suddenly seems to him that he only dreamt it, a semi-legible letter demanding that Anan be arrested because his followers had unlawfully declared the rabbi, who'd emerged from Persia's sect-ridden interior, to be the exarch over the Babylonian congregation. Al-Mansur has Anan ben David thrown into the squalid cell which already houses Abu Khanifa. The colossal gaoler leads Anan ben David to a tiny iron door, barred by two oak beams, which barely reaches to his hip, opens it, forces the rabbi to his knees and sends him into the cell with a mighty kick. For a long while the rabbi lies senseless on the stone floor. Coming to, he gradually makes out the cell in which he finds himself, square, high and narrow. The only source of light is a small barred window somewhere above him in the rough-hewn wall, unreachable. A figure cowers in one corner. Anan ben David crawls up to it, recognizes Abu Khanifa, crawls back, cowering down in the corner diagonally opposite the Muslim's. The two theologians are silent, each believing the other to be in the wrong, not towards al-Mansur, who has treated both of them shamefully, but as far as the eternal truth is concerned. Every day an ancient gaoler, who for the sake of peace and quiet passes himself off as a Sabian but actually worships a rusty one-eyed idol and despises Muslims, Jews and Christians as godless asses, silently sets before them a bowl of food and a jug of wine. The food is cooked to perfection, at the behest of al-Mansur, whose cruelty is never base, always exquisite—the insult to both lies in the fact that Jew and Muslim must eat from the same bowl; the wine insults only Abu Khanifa. For a week the theologians eat nothing. Steadfast to the point of excess, each seeks to be the most devout, shaming his opponent with his submission to God's will. They both sample only the wine, moistening their lips now and then—the Muslim so as not to die of thirst, which would also have been a sin against Allah, and the Jew, for whom wine is permitted, so as not to seem cruel towards Abu Khanifa whose thirst he would redouble if he drank deeply. Rats pounce upon the bowl of food, rats are everywhere, they venture out timidly at first, then turn bolder by the day. After a week's time Abu Khanifa is outraged by the Jew's humility, which can't possibly be true humility like his, the Muslim's; the Jew must be acting out of blasphemous defiance or diabolical malice with the intent to humiliate the servant of the Prophet, the profound scholar of the Koran, the Sunna, the Hadith through feigned humility—Abu Khanifa empties the bowl in a flash before the rats can pounce upon it again as usual, quick though the beasts may be. The theologian leaves behind just a small residue which Anan ben David laps up, humbly, with downcast eyes, though not entirely without haste, too frantic is his hunger, but he thinks upon the Talmud, which rejects martyrdom, and now the disappointed rats beset him, indeed, they snap at him. Suddenly, like an epiphany, Abu Khanifa realizes that the Jew's humility is genuine. Shamed by this, shattered, contrite before Allah, the next day it is Abu Khanifa who eats nothing, while Anan ben David, for his part loath to humiliate Abu Khanifa, who had eaten the previous day, and convinced of his piety and moreover humiliated by the Muslim's humility towards him and Jehovah, empties the bowl, devours—such is his haste—bolts down all the delectable dishes, more hastily still than Abu Khanifa the day before, for the rats have grown still greedier, still cheekier, still more rambunctious, but like the Muslim before him, he only almost empties it, so that Abu Khanifa, glad that he can finally humiliate himself before the rabbi in the same fashion, can lap up the rest, he too crawling with rats now, indeed piled with them, flooded, one can hardly tell now what is Abu Khanifa and what are rats. In time the beasts withdraw, resentful and bitterly disappointed. From then on both, the Muslim and the Jew, cower contentedly across from one another in equal piety, both equally humiliated, both equally humble, both equally exhausted by the pious duel. They have convinced each other, not through their belief, which remains different in each, irreconcilable, but through their equally matched piety, through the same mighty force with which they believe their differing beliefs. Thus begins a theological dialogue, abetted by the moonlight whose glare slants through the barred hole of a window. The two speak together, at first hesitantly, cautiously, interrupted by long spells of the profoundest absorption, now Abu Khanifa asks and Anan ben David replies, now the rabbi asks and the Muslim replies. Dawn breaks, somewhere the torturers are already at work. The screams and groans make conversation impossible; Rabbi Anan and Abu Khanifa pray so loudly and forcefully, each in his own language, that the startled torturers let up on their victims. Day comes, the sun blazes into the cell, razor sharp, a ray of light, though it fails to reach the floor of the cell, for a bare moment lighting Abu Khanifa's white hair. Day follows day, night follows night, together they eat but what is necessary, but little of the food which grows worse and worse as the caliph's command is gradually forgotten. Instead of wine, the jug has long held water. In the end the wordless gaoler tosses them an indefinable mush whose remains they leave to the rats, now their friends, piping amiably about them and rubbing their noses against them. The two men pet them absently, so engrossed are they in their mighty dialogue. The Muslim and the Jew praise the same majestic God and find it miraculous beyond all measure that He should have revealed Himself in two books at once, in the Bible and in the Koran, more obscurely in the Bible, unpredictable in His mercy and His wrath, in His inconceivable injustice which always turns out to be justice in disguise, more poetically in the Koran, more hymnic and somewhat more practical in his commandments. But as the two theologians praise God they gradually begin to deplore the human folly of adding to the original divine scriptures—Anan ben David curses the Talmud, Abu Khanifa the Sunna and the Hadith. Years pass. The caliph has long since forgotten the two theologians. He barely takes note when his intelligence service reports the spread of the belief that the Koran alone has validity, perhaps this new faith can be put to political use some day, one way or another, and when the Jewish minister of Jewish affairs tries to report that doubts in the legitimacy of the Talmud are spreading among the Jews of Babylonia, he breaks off his presentation because of al-Mansur's excessive yawning. With advancing age, al-Mansur is taxed by his harem more than by his enormous realm, the eunuchs are already cracking jokes; besides, the grand vizier isn't to be trusted. Sensing that the caliph no longer trusts him, the grand vizier forgets the two prisoners as well, with a clear conscience, it being the task of the administrators to look after Anan ben David and Abu Khanifa. But the administrators are overwhelmed, the prison far too small given the political turmoil that commences—slave revolts, Mazdak communist rebellions, one harem after the other defects to their side, for they also have their women in common. New prisons are built, first alongside the old one, using its outer walls as supporting walls for further oubliettes, an entire prison city takes form over which, in time, a second and a third prison city rises, unplanned but solid, block piled on block. Al-Mansur is long dead and his successor al-Mahdi and his successor al-Hadi ibn al-Mahdi, whom his mother had assassinated to put her favourite son Harun al-Rashid ibn al-Mahdi into power; then he dies and his successor and so on, all of them sink into nothingness. The prison where Abu Khanifa and Anan ben David cower across from each other, deep below all the prisons built next to it and over it and next to these and over these, because the revolt of the Negro slaves forced the caliph al-Mutamid ibn al-Mutawakkil to build vast new prisons, this cell of just a few square yards in the original prison is long since buried and with it Abu Khanifa and Anan ben David, though neither of them is aware of it, still sitting across from each other in the darkness, almost in the darkness, for by day, filtering through the countless criss-crossing shafts, result of the endless construction process, a faint glimmer of light filters down to them, just enough for them to make out each other's faces if they lean towards each other. But that does not concern them, the subject that occupies them is inexhaustible, indeed seems to grow more inexhaustible the deeper they immerse themselves in it. Their subject is God in His sublimity, against which everything is insignificant—the wretched food, the damp fur of the rats who have long since devoured the Koran and the Torah, the only two books which al-Mansur was forced to allow them as prison reading. They haven't even noticed that they no longer possess these sacred treasures—Abu Khanifa and Anan ben David stroked the beasts' fur tenderly as they began their work of destruction. One could say that Abu Khanifa has long since become the Koran and Anan ben David the Torah; when the Jew recites a passage from the Torah, the Arab recites a sura from the Koran which speaks to the Torah passage. Mysteriously, the two books seem to complement each other; though there is no agreement in their wording, they agree nonetheless. The two prisoners' peace is absolute but in their absorption in the divine revelations which seem to contradict, yet in fact complement, each other, there is one thing they fail to reckon with, with their closest neighbour, the gaoler, the Sabian grown hoary as they, who still secretly worships his idol and despises the Arab and the Jew the more truculently the more remorseless is the silence of the crude one-eyed idol. Like them, he has been forgotten long ago, the prison administration no longer knows of his existence, he must beg for his food from other gaolers who have also been forgotten and must beg for their food in turn. What little the Sabian begs for, he mechanically shares with the prisoners, acting on a certain sense of duty that is stronger than his contempt for them, a contempt that gradually turns to hatred, to a dark impotent rage that gnaws at him, filling him until in truth he is nothing more than this hatred towards all Jews and Arabs and beyond that towards their God who is supposed to have spoken once upon a time, this poet god, as he calls him, without actually knowing where he picked up the word, for he doesn't know what a poet is supposed to be either. And then some caliph, be it al-Qadir ibn Ishaq ibn al-Muqtadir or al-Qaim ibn al-Qadir, following a blissful night of love with a Venetian captive by the name of Amanda, Anunciata or Annabella with long cinnabar hair, orders the release of all prisoners whose names begin with A. Two hundred years later, in the final days of al-Mustansir ibn az-Zahir, the next to last of all the caliphs, the order chances to reach the ancient Sabian who grumblingly releases Anan ben David, albeit with some hesitation, feeling that he ought to release Abu Khanifa as well, he could go by the 'Abu', he thinks, and no one would notice, but his hatred towards the two moves him to go by the 'Khanifa' instead and separate the two theologians. And so, with malicious pleasure, he releases only Anan ben David. Distraught, the Jew takes his leave from Abu Khanifa, runs his fingers once more over his dear friend's face, gazes into his eyes, which seem to be made of stone, and feels all at once that Abu Khanifa is no longer aware of this parting, that he has lost all sense of change. Then he stumbles in a daze down dark corridors, seized by a vague fear of freedom, climbs ladders that lead up wet walls to further prisons, blunders down ever-new corridors, reaches steep stairs and suddenly finds himself in the glaring sunlight of a courtyard, blinking, old, unspeakably filthy, in rags. Seeing, like a kind of salvation, that half the courtyard lies in shadow, he shuts his eyes, gropes his way to the wall, sinks down against it. A gaoler or prison official finds him, questions him, understands nothing, unlocks the prison gate for him, shaking his head. The old man doesn't want to leave his place by the wall, the gaoler (or prison official) threatens to use force, the old man must obey. Thus begins Anan ben David's endless wanderings through the world, unwilling wanderings, for hardly is he outside the prison gate, hardly among people, that all of them stare at him; he is dressed differently than they, in tattered, filthy rags, but in antiquated clothing. His Arabic sounds different, too; when he asks for a certain street, no one understands him, and besides this street no longer exists, the city has changed; a few mosques look vaguely familiar. He seeks the Jewish congregation, reports to the rabbi, a renowned Talmud expert. Here, too, people have trouble understanding the ancient Anan ben David, but they admit him to the holy man who is studying the Arabic book of the famous Rabbi Saadia ben Joseph: *The Refutation of Anan*. The ancient little manikin, hair gone ice-grey, clutches the knees of the great Talmudist, names his name. Flabbergasted, the rabbi asks him again, turns severe, calls Anan ben David either a fool or an imposter, the real Rabbi Anan died nearly five hundred years ago and was a heretic besides, polluted by esoteric

Persian doctrines, he'd best be getting on his way. Then he
turns back to his book. Anan ben David's ancient face
flushes: Does he still believe in the Talmud, then, he asks
the rabbi, that sorry work of man? Now the renowned Talmud expert rises, a giant with a wild pitch-black beard, not
for nothing does the congregation call him the 'holy colossus'. 'Begone, thou wretched ghost of Anan ben David,' he
thunders, 'thou long-decayed one! Leave me and my congregation in peace. While you lived, you led us into ruin,
and now may you be accursed as one long since buried!'
Appalled, Anan ben David rushes from the holy man's house
as the Jew's curses ring out after him. He blunders aimlessly
through the vast city's streets and across its squares. Street
urchins throw stones at him, dogs snap at him, a drunk
pushes him to the ground. He has no idea what to do but
report back to the prison gate which he finds with great difficulty. Bewildered officials open the gate, but no one
remembers him, the prison official (or gaoler) who released
him is nowhere to be found. The old Jew describes Abu
Khanifa, but no one has ever heard of such a prisoner. A
young sub-director in the general administration of all the
city's prisons takes a historical interest in the Jew. The name
Abu Khanifa is vaguely familiar to him; although it's probably a mix-up on the part of the Jew, there must be some
truth to the tale. He assigns the old man a cell in the new
prison complex, originally intended for wealthy pre-trial
detainees, with a view of the Harun-al-Rashid Mosque, has
him fed and given new clothes. The sub-director is surprised
by his own generosity. He delves into old directories, exam-
ines old blueprints but nothing suggests that beneath all the
prison buildings yet another prison might be found—in a
sense, the primal prison. The sub-director summons old
gaolers, ancient ones, long since retired, but no one has ever

heard of a Sabian gaoler. Of course no one knows the entire prison, admittedly the blueprints are incomplete, but some trace would have to exist if there were any truth to the old Jew's account. This the sub-director owns at last, sorrowfully, for he believes the Jew somehow, feels an obligation towards him, strange, he admits it, feels irresolute, asks the director if the old man couldn't be provided with a cell, best of all the cell where he already lives, with the view of the mosque. Unfortunately that's out of the question, says the director, rather piqued at his sub-director, who can't possibly be serious in assuming some connection between the old Jew and Abu Khanifa who has been dead for hundreds of years. He's a prison director and not the head of a lunatic asylum, which is exactly where the sub-director should have the Jew committed. But with this decision reached, Anan ben David has vanished. No one can say how he managed to leave his cell, perhaps it was unlocked, perhaps the gaoler found the Jew dead on his cot and had the corpse removed without reporting the trifling incident. But fifteen years later, when Hülägu, a grandson of Genghis Khan, burns down the city with its mosques, hospitals and libraries, butchers eight hundred thousand inhabitants and has the versifying al-Mustasim ibn az-Zahir, an Abbasid and a paragon of gentleness, rolled in a carpet and shaken to death, to avoid, superstitious as the Mongol is, angering the soil of the conquered Abbasid realm with the blood of the last caliph, a cataphract sees an ancient, stooped little Jew escape from an incinerated synagogue and, amazed that anyone there has survived, sends an arrow in his direction, unable to swear, in the uncertain smoky light, whether he had hit his mark. Two hundred years later, in Granada, a nondescript Jew of uncertain age approaches the head of the Jewish congregation, who can barely understand him, at last realizing that the old man wants to discuss something with Rabbi Moses ben Maimon and responding kindly that the 'Rambam' died nearly three hundred years ago in Cairo, whereupon the stranger withdraws in shock. In the first years of Karl V's reign as king of Spain, an old Jewish man falls into the hands of the Inquisition and is presented to the grand inquisitor as a curiosity. The Jew does not answer questions, it is impossible to determine whether he is mute. For a long while the grand inquisitor is silent, staring at the Jew almost reverently, then motions vaguely with his hand, letting him go as one already moribund. We do not know whether all these reports are of Anan ben David, the only thing certain is that he roams the world without ever again revealing himself, that he does not speak his name. He wanders from one land to the next, from one Jewish congregation to the next, and says not another word. In the synagogues, he drapes himself in a tattered old prayer shawl; like the grand inquisitor, people take him to be deaf and dumb. Now he crops up in this ghetto, now in that one, now cowering in this beth midrash, now in that. No one pays him any mind, he's just the old deaf-and-dumb Jew who's come from somewhere or other, to whom a few necessities are doled out, whom each generation knows but takes for someone else, who looks like some other ancient, deaf-and-dumb Jew the older generation supposedly knew. And, indeed, he's as good as nothing, a mere shadow, a memory, a legend; what he needs is a little bread, a little water, a little wine, a little schnapps, as the case may be, he just sips at it anyway, staring into space with his huge eyes, not even nodding in thanks. Probably dotty, senile. And he doesn't care what people think of him, where he finds himself, the persecutions, the pogroms don't touch him, he's so old now that none of the enemies of his people molest him; the grand inquisitor was the last to take notice of him. Anan ben David has long since gone to ground in Eastern Europe, for years he spends the winter stoking the stoves at the school of the great Maggid of Mezeritch, a Chassidic legend, perhaps; where he spends the summers, no one can report. Finally, in the Second World War, a Nazi doctor selects him from a long line of naked Jews moving towards a gas chamber in Auschwitz; he fancies a few experiments with the little old man, freezes him, five, ten, fifteen hours at a hundred below, two weeks, two months, the Jew is still alive, thinking about something or other, never really there; the doctor gives up. Not wanting to send him back, he leaves him in peace, now and then ordering him to clean the lab. All at once the Jew has vanished and already the Nazi has forgotten him. But as the centuries sink away, the centuries spent in prison with Abu Khanifa, in that wretched Baghdad cell, grow more and more significant for Anan ben David, more powerful, more radiant. To be sure, he has long since forgotten Abu Khanifa, he imagines that he was alone in the dark dungeon where al-Mansur had him thrown (he has forgotten his name as well), but now it seems to him that he spent all those endless years speaking with Yahweh, and not only speaking, feeling His breath, even seeing His immeasurable face, so that the wretched hole that held him captive seems more and more like the Promised Land and all his thinking concentrates on this one place like light in a focus and becomes an overwhelming yearning to go back there, back to that holy place, indeed that he is still alive only because within him is this yearning to return and nothing but, though admittedly he has long since forgotten where in fact that holy place is, just as he has forgotten Abu Khanifa—who meanwhile, still cowering in his cell, turned by the occasional falling water droplets into a kind of stalagmite with a spark of life, likewise forgot Anan ben David centuries ago, just as the old Sabian has forgotten Abu Khanifa; he came less and less frequently and finally stopped coming at all. Perhaps the one-eyed, rusty idol killed him, falling from the wall. But Abu Khanifa's bowl is not left empty; the rats, the only living creatures who know their way about the prisons piled and jumbled together, bring him the little he needs for his nourishment. Their lives are brief, but the solicitude for the forgotten prisoner is handed down, he has been their friend for countless rat generations, he shared his food with them once and now they share theirs with him. But he takes their ministrations for granted, barely stroking their fur now and then, more and more rarely the more he turns to stone, for his thoughts are elsewhere—to him, too, it seems that he spent centuries speaking with Allah, alone in this dark dungeon, and the wretched cell in which he cowers has long ceased to be a cell for him. He forgot the caliph long ago, sometimes making an effort to remember the name, the trifling disagreement for which he went to prison—he can't even remember what this dispute was about, nor does he realize that he could actually have left the prison long ago, that no one would detain him. He is filled by the certainty of sojourning in a holy place, lit now and then only faintly, rough-hewn blocks of stone, glimmering in the dark, but hallowed by Him with Whom he spoke, by Allah Himself; and what keeps him alive is the task of tending this place, through his perseverance, as his, Abu Khanifa's property, consigned to him by Allah Himself. And so Abu Khanifa waits for the hour when Allah in His mercy will speak to him again, when he will feel His breath again and see His immeasurable face. He awaits this hour with all the yearning of his heart, with the ardent force of his spirit, and this hour looms, though differently than imagined.

Anan ben David's odysseys have taken him to Istanbul, by chance, he doesn't even know that he's in Istanbul. For weeks he crouches outside an old synagogue, almost one with its walls, grey and weathered like its stones, until a Swiss drunk discovers him, a sculptor who, when not drunk, welds together massive iron machines and blocks. The Swiss fellow stares at the ancient little dwarf-like Jew, slings him over his mighty shoulders and lugs him to a rusty, patched-together Volkswagen van. Actually, in Istanbul, the Swiss isn't really drunk yet, just tipsy, but then more drunk by the stop en route through Anatolia; evidently, he's trying to smuggle whisky in his van to earn money for his iron sculptures, and he seems to have a knack for it, though the whisky dwindles alarmingly and with it the profits—at each border post, at each police station, at each checkpoint he generously produces the whisky and an endless party begins, with the result that the border posts, the police stations and checkpoints end up even more drunk than the Swiss. Each time, Anan ben David, still playing mute, attested with a shake of his head that whisky is not prohibited by the Koran, which is why the Swiss took him along, taking the ancient creature for a Muslim, a connection which does not occur to Anan ben David, immersed in Yahweh and anticipating a reunion with him. But in Baghdad, without Anan ben David knowing that he's in Baghdad, believing himself to be in Argen-tina or Vladivostok, such is the confusion of continents and memories in his mind after centuries of roaming, in Baghdad the Swiss hurtles into a traffic island going over hundred and twenty kilometres per hour where sixty is . . . traffic island, traffic policeman, sculptor and van are ablaze with gas and whisky flames, everything explodes, goes up in a yellow pillar of Old Smuggler smoke along with one of the great white hopes of Helvetia's art scene. But Anan ben

David vanishes in the gathering crowd that prevents the honking police cars and ambulances from making headway—all that's left of the Swiss is a hand that seems to swear an oath; to what, can no longer be said. Anan ben David hurries along past luxury boutiques, ducking round a highrise when he notices a white dog following him, long-legged and bald, its fur fallen out. Anan ben David flees into a narrow side street, the houses are ancient or so dilapidated they seem ancient, though the high-rise must be quite near, even if it's no longer visible. Anan ben David no longer sees the dog but knows it's following him. He opens the door of an old, derelict house, enters a courtyard filled with rubble, clambers over it, finds an opening in the ground, half wellshaft, half cave. A rat stares at him malignly, the bald white dog appears in the door of the house, bares its teeth. Anan ben David climbs down into the cave, gropes for stairs, climbs down, finds himself in endless corridors, in total blackness, but he walks on. He knows that the bald white dog is slinking in pursuit, that the rats are waiting for him. Suddenly he feels at home, a familiarity, he stops. He knows, without seeing it, that there's an abyss at his feet, he bends down, his hands grasp empty space, then a ladder, he climbs down, fearless, reaches solid ground, a new abyss, again his hands grope in the void, all at once there's a new ladder. He climbs down, the ladder swaying, the dog yelping above him. Remembering the way now, he walks down the low corridors, finds the low iron door, the beams have rotted, the door is so rusty that it turns to dust when he touches it; he crawls into the Promised Land—into his cell, his dungeon, his prison, his oubliette where he spoke with Yahweh, to the rough undressed blocks, the damp ground. He sits himself down. An infinite peace descends upon him, the peace of his God, the peace of Yahweh. But suddenly two hands close round his neck. Abu Khanifa assaults him as though Anan ben David were a wild animal, a beast that has invaded his, Abu Khanifa's realm, which belongs to Allah, and Abu Khanifa is animated solely by the sacred duty to kill this intruder who threatens his freedom—for his freedom consists not only in the fact that this wretched cell is his cell, Abu Khanifa's cell, but also that it was created by Allah as his, Abu Khanifa's, cell. Meanwhile Anan ben David defends himself with equal fury—the attacker has taken possession of his, Anan ben David's, Promised Land, of the place where He, Yahweh, spoke with him, His unworthy servant, where he felt His breath, beheld His immeasurable face. The struggle is brutal, without mercy; each defends, in his freedom, the freedom of his God to ordain a place for those who believe in Him. And the struggle is all the harder for Anan ben David as countless rats assail him, fastening onto him, rabid, bloodthirsty. Exhausted, the two combatants back down, Anan ben David at the end of his strength; he knows a new attack by his opponent and the rats will be too much for him. But then little by little, hesitantly at first, the rats who'd attacked Anan ben David, these fearsome beasts, nestle up to him and lick his wounds; with the hereditary instinct of countless generations they have recognized him, and as they lick him he senses the immediate presence of Yahweh, his God, he leans forward involuntarily to make out his foe in the dim uncertain light, and his foe leans towards him, laboriously, shattering the calcareous sandstone that encases him like armour, shattered already as his hatred just now cracked it. Anan ben David stares into Abu Khanifa's face and Abu Khanifa into Anan ben David's—each, grown ancient over the countless centuries, stares at himself, their faces are the same. But gradually the hatred drains from their eyes, stony, nearly blind; they stare at each other as they stared at their

God, at Yahweh and Allah, and for the first time their lips, silent for so long, for millennia, form the first word, not a saying from the Koran, not a word from the Pentateuch, just the word: You. Anan ben David recognizes Abu Khanifa and Abu Khanifa recognizes Anan ben David. Yahweh was Abu Khanifa and Allah was Anan ben David—their struggle for freedom was an absurdity. Abu Khanifa's fossilized mouth forms a smile; hesitantly, almost diffidently, as though touching a sacred object, Anan ben David runs his fingers through his friend's white hair. Abu Khanifa grasps, faced with the ancient little Jew who squats before him, and Anan ben David perceives, faced with the Arab who cowers before him on the tiles of the dungeon, that their shared possession, the prison of Abu Khanifa and the dungeon of Anan ben David, is the freedom of the one and the freedom of the other.

I have many names. So many that I remember none of them, and because they gave me so many names they believed me to have a thousand forms, a million forms, probably even more, but I've never been interested in numbers; later they reduced me to a One, after all it's easier to reckon with one than with many; they thought up a complicated theory according to which this One is actually three, but I'm just mentioning it in passing, I never understood it. I say 'they'. I don't know what I mean by it. Evidently, something outside myself. I can't imagine something outside myself. Nor Me, Mine and I. I can't imagine myself. I'm not imaginable, I'm only thinkable, and even the most nonsensical things are thinkable. I am the most nonsensical thing. A non-sense. I am not I, and I am I. I exist, and I do not exist. I am a point, a straight line, a plane, a cube, a sphere, an n-dimensional solid and none of these things, Nothing. I am omnipotent and powerless, omniscient and oblivious, I am all that they claim me to be, because it doesn't matter what they claim, and so I keep arriving at this 'they'. I created them once, or they were once I, at one time before the moment that is now, I don't know how long before, perhaps immediately before or just now, it makes no difference in eternity. Perhaps everything is just an idea of mine, a thought that struck me, strikes or will strike, no matter, whenever, having once struck, in the past perfect, in the past, in the present, in the future, in the future perfect, on the far side of all infinity, the thought would grow beyond measure and collapse again to nothingness. Endlessness and nothingness are the same, and so I am identical with what I have created, am creating or will create, or have not created, am not creating or will not create. Possibly among these things created, real or imaginary, in this 'creation', to wax pompous, there is something which thinks, which, because the I that I adopt from linguistic convenience also thinks, can only be identical with me. Possibly this I of thought which I myself am is thinking me, out of sheer despair at the inability to escape itself or in the delusion of finding itself a meaning. Possibly I will burst into laughter, a redoubled laughter, it being exceedingly funny to imagine something that can't be imagined bursting into laughter because it pictures something bursting into laughter, so that laughter follows laughter without end. But perhaps I am thinkable only as something comical, something grotesque, purely as a joke, as a joke per se, as a punchline without a story, concluding without connecting, a conclusion without a premise, dissolving in the nothingness of laughter. Perhaps I am laughter per se, laughter without cause, being without cause myself and thus without meaning, as it is meaningless to seek meaning behind something causeless. But this possible I of thought—and what in this possible creation, be it real or imaginary, is not possible—will have to love or hate me, I who am itself. Both are equally indecent. If it loves me, it will sacrifice itself, for one sacrifices oneself only for something which one fails to comprehend and which one can lend meaning only through sacrifice. If it hates me, it will consume itself, for one consumes oneself only over a being which one can give meaning only by hating it. But since love and hate will be too hard, it will merely chatter about me, for one can only chatter about something whose meaning is irrelevant. Only those who chatter about me are not indecent. I am one with the chatter about me. I am chatter. I exist only insofar as I chatter. If I didn't chatter, I'd take myself seriously; if I took myself seriously, I'd have to have a meaning; if I had a meaning, I'd have to have a cause. What is causeless has no meaning, again and again I come back to these words, in which my creation, if I did create it, balloons and deflates again, as meaningless as I who created it. If I created it, I will never know, because memory has no value in meaninglessness. But when I think over the possibility that I could have created, could be creating, could one day create something outside myself, a creation, and as this possibility would encompass all possibilities, past, present and future, including that of the thought identical with myself, this thought, no matter who its thinker is, would, even if my laughter at it fades (if it is even capable of fading), seek the author of its self, even if it knew how to do without meaning. It cannot do without a cause. It will imagine that the cause lies in me, that only I know the meaning of its existence. But as I do not exist, it will have to invent me. It will call this invention belief; and as its belief has no fixed object, it will invent me endlessly, name me with endless names, it will believe me to exist in a thousand, a million forms or reduce me to three, to one, to an idea, to a principle, finally to nothingness, to the one true belief that I do not exist. But this belief, which suspends belief, will not be believed, they will believe once again that I am in fact a principle, an idea, a one, a three, many forms, a thousand forms, a million forms—once I am thought, I am thought; only when I am no longer thought am I what I am—nothing.

SOURCES

• 'From the Beginning'
Originally published as 'Vom Anfang her' (1957) in *Literatur und Kunst* (Zurich: Diogenes Verlag, 1998), pp. 11–12.

• 'Document'
Originally published as 'Dokument' (1965) in *Literatur und Kunst* (Zurich: Diogenes Verlag, 1998), pp. 13–25.

• 'Vallon de l'Ermitage'
Originally published as 'Vallon de l'Ermitage' (1980) in *Versuche / Kants Hoffnung* (Zurich: Diogenes Verlag, 1998), pp. 11–58.

• 'Personal Remarks on My Pictures and Drawings'
Originally published as 'Persönliche Anmerkungen zu meinen Bildern und Zeichnungen' (1978) in *Literatur und Kunst* (Zurich: Diogenes Verlag, 1998), pp. 201–16.

• 'Finger Exercises on the Present'
Originally published as 'Fingerübungen zur Gegenwart' (1952) in *Literatur und Kunst* (Zurich: Diogenes Verlag, 1998), pp. 31–2.

• 'Theorems on the Theatre'
Originally published as 'Sätze über das Theater' (1970) in *Theater* (Zurich: Digenes Verlag, 1998), pp. 176–211.

• 'Aspects of Dramaturgical Thinking: Fragment'
Originally published as 'Aspekte des dramaturgischen Denkens: Fragment' (1964) in *Theater* (Zurich: Digenes Verlag, 1998), pp. 104–20.

• 'Note on Comedy'
Originally published as 'Anmerkung zur Komödie' (1952) in *Theater* (Zurich: Digenes Verlag, 1998), pp. 20–5.

• 'American and European Drama'

Originally published as 'Amerikanisches und europäisches Drama' (1959) in *Theater* (Zurich: Digenes Verlag, 1998), pp. 78–83.

• 'Georg Büchner and the Principle of Cause'

Originally published as 'Georg Büchner und der Satz vom Grunde' (1986) in *Versuche / Kants Hoffnung* (Zurich: Diogenes Verlag, 1998), pp. 59–71.

• 'Art and Science; or, Plato; or, Creativity, Vision and Idea; or, A Difficult Form of Address; or, Beginning and End of a Public Address'

Originally published as 'Kunst und Wissenschaft oder; Platon; oder Einfall, Vision und Idee oder; Die Schwierigkeit einer Anrede; oder Anfang und Ende einer Rede' (1984) in *Versuche / Kants Hoffnung* (Zurich: Diogenes Verlag, 1998), pp. 72–97.

• 'Humanity's Fate'

Originally published as 'Das Schicksal der Menschen' (1950) in *Politik* (Zurich: Digenes Verlag, 1998), pp. 15–19.

• 'On Tolerance'

Originally published as 'Über Toleranz' (1977) in *Philosophie und Natur-wissenschaft* (Zurich: Digenes Verlag, 1998), pp. 125–49.

• 'Abu Khanifa and Anan ben David'

Originally published as 'Abu Chanifa und Anan ben David' (1975) in *Der Sturz / Abu Chanifa und Anan ben David / Smithy / Das Sterben Der Pythia* (Zurich: Diogenes Verlag, 1998), pp. 65–86.

• 'Monologue'

Originally published as 'Selbstgespräch (1985) in *Versuche / Kants Hoff-nung* (Zurich: Diogenes Verlag, 1998), pp. 115–18.